Under Suffolk Skies Series
WALKS IN SUFFOLK

2.
River & Coastal Walks In Suffolk

Written and Compiled by Mel Birch
with illustrations by Julie Hawkins

PUBLISHED BY IMAGES PUBLICATIONS, STOWMARKET, SUFFOLK

RIVER & COASTAL WALKS IN SUFFOLK

OTHER PUBLICATIONS FROM IMAGES
Include:
EATING OUT IN SUFFOLK
EATING OUT IN NORFOLK
OUT & ABOUT IN SUFFOLK — COUNTY GUIDE
HISTORIC WALKS IN NORFOLK
IMAGES OF SUFFOLK
HISTORIC EAST ANGLIA IN CAMERA

First Printed 1985
Reprinted 1987
Second reprint 1988
Third reprint 1989
Fourth reprint 1990

The Rights of Way described in this publication were correct, to the best of our knowledge, at the time of going to press. We cannot accept responsibility for damage, trespass or nuisance caused by others in the course of negotiating the walks herein described or for errors due to rerouting or closing of footpaths or misunderstood directions.

CONTENTS

Your Starting Points

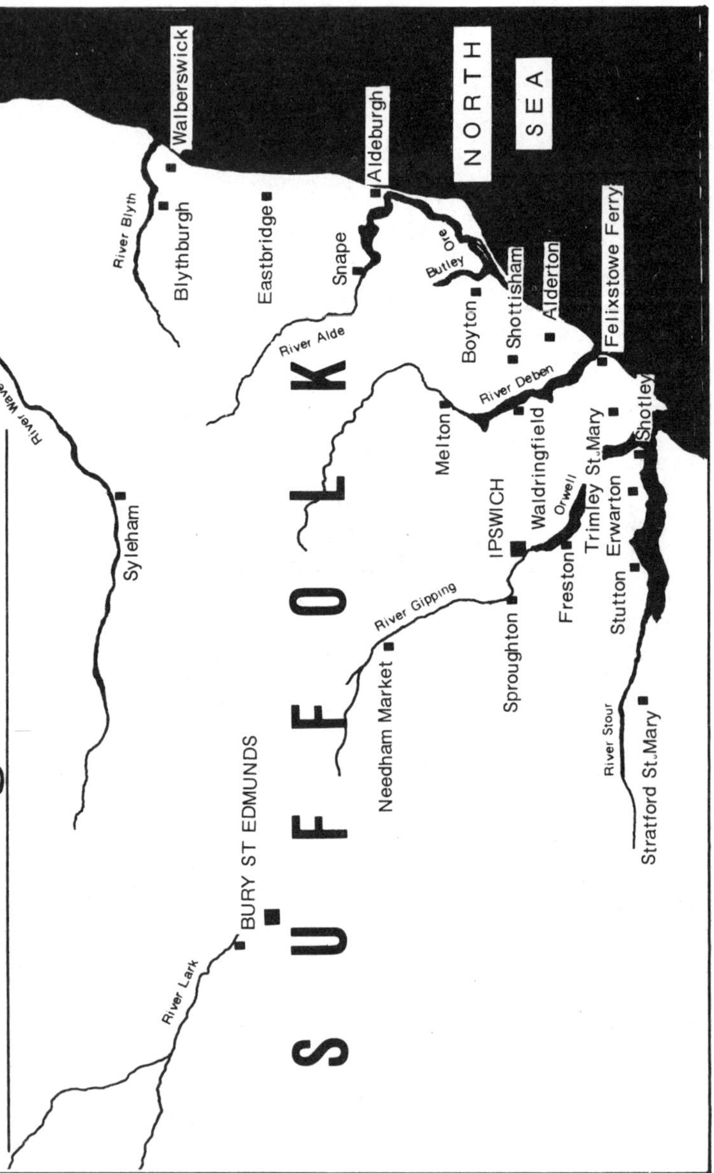

An Introduction

River & Coastal *is the second in a series of four Suffolk Walk books.*

My aims in these publications are two-fold; firstly to provide the opportunity for healthy exercise whilst experiencing the pleasure of an ever changing country-side and, secondly, to present to you the many facets which go to make up Suffolk's endearing appeal.

The initial book, **Historic Walks In Suffolk,** *took you on twenty excursions to historic sites in the county, some well-known, others less so - due mainly to their unaccessability by road. I hope they provided many new and exciting discoveries.*

In **River & Coastal** *I shall introduce you to an aspect of the county few really appreciate. Suffolk is one of England's most maritime counties, being bordered on two sides by rivers and on the east by the North Sea. In addition, there are two other major rivers running through the heart of the county and several less grand, but still with their own personality and history.*

The Orwell is now unquestionably the most important waterway, linking as it does the county town and major port of Ipswich with the Continent.

The Stour is really two rivers in one; its early course passes through the beautiful Dedham Vale on the Essex and Suffolk borders, where it has been immortalised in the paintings of John Constable, but having freed itself at Manningtree and with its own Continental Ferry Port at Harwich in sight, it throws back its banks and becomes the counties largest river, a mile wide in places, twice that of the Orwell.

The eerie marshes and mud-flats bordering the Deben evoke the perfect atmosphere for a river so steeped in history; the whole antiquity of Suffolk had its roots here. Traces of the ancient East Anglian Kingdom of the Wuffingas lie scattered along its banks while the world-famous Sutton Hoo Treasure Ship was dragged from its shores to ritual burial in a tumulus overlooking the waters.

The Waveney forms the border with Norfolk, its tranquil course passing through the scenes of woodland, pasture and water-meadow more readily associated with the county. Yet it has its moments; at Oulton Broad it becomes part of the Broads and takes the holiday cruisers on into Norfolk.

Of those less grand yet playing a still vital role in our heritage, the Gipping is no doubt satisfied at having given birth to the Orwell at Ipswich; the Blyth provides on its bank one of the most unforgettable sights on the Ipswich to Lowestoft road, Blythburgh Church; the calm open waters of the Ore and Butley rivers were created in the main by the shingle spit which destroyed the port at Orford; the Alde, on whose bank stands the famous Concert Hall at Snape Maltings, has given inspiration to poet and composer; and the Lark, near Bury St Edmunds, keeps memories of a terrible carnage in its waters one fateful day in 1173.

Along the 45 miles of coastline stretching from Corton in the north to Felixstowe in the south, the North Sea has held the destiny of every town and village, treating all with faint regard to wealth and favour.

While today the port of Felixstowe plays an ever increasing role in world trade, in medieval times, when the town itself did not even exist, this role was played by others with equal fervour. Their names seem so unlikely today yet Walberswick, Blythburgh, Dunwich, Orford and others were all trading ports, had flourishing fishing industries, built ships and sailed in them to fight for king and country. Their greatest battle however, was with the sea on which they depended; as we shall see, in every case this was a battle they were to lose.

As the North Sea remapped the coast, Dunwich, once the capital city of East Anglia, was lost beneath the waves, and a large part of Aldeburgh was washed away to be dumped in a shingle spit farther down the coast at Orford, cutting off that busy port from the sea and leaving its great castle as a lone reminder of its former glory.

Others turn different faces to the elements. Southwold, prim and neat hides its fear with an almost arrogant air, but at stark and windswept Shingle Street, the continual conflict with the sea is not so easily disguised.

Such a wealth of history and mood, such a stock of melancholy memories. I hope like me, you will experience them all in the course of these twenty-one walks.

Always follow the COUNTRY CODE

- REMEMBER TO CLOSE ALL GATES BEHIND YOU
- KEEP DOGS ON A LEAD
- GUARD AGAINST ALL RISK OF FIRE
- LEAVE LIVESTOCK AND MACHINERY WELL ALONE
- TAKE YOUR LITTER HOME
- PROTECT WILD LIFE, PLANTS AND TREES
- MAKE NO UNNECESSARY NOISE

Suffolk's Major Rivers

THE ORWELL: Formed at a point near Stoke Bridge in Ipswich where the river Gipping, flowing from Stowmarket, meets the sea waters and becomes tidal.

Ipswich, the chief settlement on the river, trailed Dunwich in 1279 when it had thirty great ships to the latters eighty, but with Dunwich's decline in the Middle Ages the town built up a sizeable fleet. Its facilities were such that in the 14c. Edward III and the Black Prince fitted out 500 ships here for the Calais expedition.

Apart from giving Ipswich access to world trade and shipbuilding, the Orwell provided the town with another lucrative industry during the 19c., that of Coprolite. This fossilized animal dung was dug up in great quantities all along the Orwell/ Deben peninsula and ground down to form a fertilizer. By 1877, 10,000 tons were being shipped each year - the industry is remembered in an Ipswich street of the same name.

At one time ships could not reach the town itself and had to lay anchor in Butterman Bay where their cargo was loaded and unloaded by barges. A central channel was dredged allowing even the largest ships to make the port.

Ipswich has always been in the forefront of British port development. When constructed in 1842, its wet dock was the largest in the country, and today, still moving with the times, it has become Britain's fourth largest container port.

Smuggling was always prevalent along such a trade conscious river as the Orwell and apart from the white cat of Woolverstone mentioned later, Pin Mill, Levington and the other little picturesque quays along the banks all have their stories to tell.

THE STOUR: Immortalised by those two great Suffolk painters, John Constable and Thomas Gainsborough, the Stour formed the ancient division between the Kingdom of East Anglia and Essex.

Although its source is in Cambridgeshire, all its three tributaries, the Glem, the Box, and the Brett, rise in Suffolk.

It is the counties largest river being over one mile wide in places and fifty miles long, the last ten being tidal.

Its largest town is Sudbury but the port of Harwich stands on the Orwell/Stour Estuary.

Wool was the greatest factor in the prosperity of the towns and villages bordering the Stour, but this great East Anglian Industry gradually declined through the latter half of the 16c. and little came to replace it.

In the reign of Queen Anne, an Act of Parliament in 1705 allowed for making the river navigable from Manningtree to Sudbury; the work started in 1708 and took five years.

THE DEBEN: Rises at Aspal near Debenham but fails to reach river status until it reaches Woodbridge; it is from here to the sea that all its ancient settlements lie.

The lower part of the Deben once formed the great open port of Goseford, the wool port of the Saxons.

While the Orwell may always have been the main entry point for invasion, the Deben proved the major attraction when it came to ancient settlement. The estuary is still haunted by the Wuffingas, the ruling house of East Anglia at the time when pagan rites were being slowly superceeded by Christian. The great Sutton Hoo ship burial dates from this time.

There were many ancient quays along the banks of the Deben; though none were large, they combined to make the river a thriving source of trade. Salt was manufactured at Hemley in salt pans both here and across the river at Sutton; cement, manufactured from a mixture of river mud and chalk, at Waldringfield until a few years before the First World War (subsequently new methods were learned from Germany and the works moved to Claydon, where it still operates today); Ramsholt had a thriving oyster industry and, as stated earlier, coprolite was discovered by the shore and many quays set up to handle the shipping, Stonner Quay being one of the largest.

Woodbridge, where the river really begins, took over from Goseford as the main port in the 15c. but with the Deben unnavigable for larger ships, soon lost all its trade to Ipswich; it accepted its destiny gracefully and remains a picturesque boating centre.

Felixstowe, only a small village in the middle of the last century, has taken over the mantle of chief rival to Ipswich. Its position at the head of the estuary gives it a positive advantage in trade with the Continent.

It is Britain's largest container port and a fine example of free enterprise.

While its port is sited, it is true, on the Orwell Estuary, it is on the Deben Estuary that the town was born in the form of Walton; roles here have been reversed, the sea having taken most of Walton leaving Felixstowe to thrive.

THE WAVENEY: Rising near Redgrave on the Suffolk/Norfolk border it takes a meandering course to form the boundary between the two counties. It meets the sea at Gorleston, when it appears that it should have been at Lowestoft, taking a strange loop away from Oulton Broad to form part of the Broads before again turning east. This loop in the boundary proved inconvenient to Government planners and the land it enclosed was loped off and given to Norfolk.

The Waveney is a river of castles, five line its banks, Framlingham, Bungay, Mettingham, Wingfield and Burgh Castle (now lost to Norfolk). It seems to have been a great attraction to the Normans as it was at Syleham, possibly near the church - itself on the banks of the river - that the notorious baron Hugh Bigod surrendered his castles of Framlingham and Bungay to Henry II.

Beccles, and its near neighbour Bungay are the two major towns along the Waveney though neither were great centres of industry.

The Waveney then, remains what it has always been, a quiet, tranquil river in keeping with the countryside through which is flows.

RIVER GIPPING

. . . . What tho' thy neighbour Orwell boast
His variegated length of coast,
His busy trade and shipping;
Tell him that happiness may stray
Where pomp could never find the way,
And glide thro' vales with Gipping.

No envious sands thy course perplex,
No howling storms thy waters vex,
Their shores of Verdure stripping;
Thy peaceful streams translucent glide,
While Flow'rets bend on either side
To view themselves in Gipping . . . .

(Elizabeth Cobbold)

NUMBER ONE - RIVER GIPPING

Places visited: *Needham Market, Great Blakenham, Darmsden, Barking, Baylham.*
Distance: *8½ miles*
Starting Point: *Needham Market Station Car Park, off High Street.*
Refreshments: *Pub, Gt.Blakenham; Restaurants, pubs and cafes, Needham.*
Map Ref: *1:25000 Pathfinder TM05/15 1:50000 Landranger Sheet 155.*

BAYLHAM MILL

THE WALK: From Needham Market station car park walk back to the main high Street. Cross to the Swan public house and turn left. At the end of the street turn right to the Barking road and immediately right again onto a well-used public footpath(SP). Carry on passing the Telephone Exchange on the left and the school playing fields on the right. At the top, cross the estate road, and continue on in the same direction along a track beside a field. A further ¼ mile brings you to a crossways of paths; go right and left to join a path bordered and enclosed by high hedging. This path which runs from Needham to Barking, and known as The Causeway, has a rather macabre history. Until 1901 Needham was only a hamlet of Barking and its church, then only a chapel, had no churchyard. Following a funeral at Needham the bodies were then wheeled in a procession the 1½ miles along the Causeway to be buried at Barking. Eventually the way swings left and then comes out into a metalled lane. Go right signposted to the church passing the rectory on the right. Go into the churchyard and visit St Mary's church which, despite an exterior not enhanced by Victorian rendering, has much of interest within, including a late c13 south porch, early Tudor carved doors and fine c14 roof.

Leave the churchyard by the far gate heading down a path beside a cultivated field to the road. Turn left and walk along the road for about 600 yards turning right at the second footpath sign. Walk up the field along a firm farm track passing between two woods and bearing left as you top the rise. Continue on along the track until you meet another crossing your path at fir trees. Turn left into this and a short way past the end of the trees turn right onto a firm, stony track heading down the valley. This is a delightful stretch and the vista of the little church of Darmsden with its bell-tower, perched on the summit of the climb beyond the valley completes the picture. Go through the green metal gates into the churchyard walking round to the right to discover the main door. Surprisingly this pretty little church of St Andrew with its fine flint work and neat proportions was rebuilt in Decorated style as recently as 1880; the Tilley lamp within emphasises its isolated situation.

Leave the church by the single gate out into a narrow country lane. Turn left and immediately bear right at the bend and then, when the lane turns left, carry straight on along a metalled drive towards the farm buildings of Roebuck Farm. The drive ends by a farm bungalow on the left and you continue on over a wide expanse of rough grass heading towards a garage on the right of another similar bungalow. Turn right here beyond the long farm building and cross rough ground skirting a lake of liquid manure on your right - it may pay to hold your nose along this section ! Turn left and make your way down the steep hill through the trees to emerge on the edge of a cultivated field. Walk up the field heading slightly right to meet a grassy track entering a wood. The track goes left and right to eventually lead you to another open field. Your way is straight on through the field following the line of a faint path. Pick up a hedge on the far side and, keeping it on your left, continue on to the crosshedge. Go through a gap in the hedge on your left here and continue on in the same direction as before through a meadow. You pass to the left of a fine flint wall and pick up a metalled drive servicing properties on both sides. Pass Glebe Cottage on the right and, on the same side, Baylham National School built in 1860 and now a private house.

At the road you can walk a few yards to the right to visit Baylham church which was considerably restored in 1870, but your route is left for a few steps then right down a green lane(SP). Descend into the valley, the hedge stopping on your right where you now have a cultivated field. Climb again and pass through a copse out onto another small country lane. Turn left, and after 75 yards right at a 'Bridleway' sign; this is misleading as there is no sign of a path here. Go over the farm gate into a meadow which you cross to a rough wooden 'stile' leading to a field. Turn half left and head up the field gradually closing on the left hand field boundary hedge. Topping the rise you should be able to make out a new footpath sign further along the left hand hedge. Bear left to head for it over the remainder of the field and follow its arrow directions through a gap in the hedge to continue along the right side of the next field with the hedge now on your right. Come out into a sunken lane and turn left. The lane becomes firmer and, with properties soon appearing on either side, later metalled,to meet the old A45 at Great Blakenham a few yards to the right of the Chequers public house where a short break for refreshments may be in order before you reach the river.

Cross the road and go down Mill Lane opposite passing the rectory. Turn left and head for the bridge over the Gipping. Turn left just before it(SP) between the appropriately named properties Gipping Weir and Bridge Weir. Follow the directions right,along a passageway beside the wall of a house. Do not go through the solid wooden gate at the end of it but left through a small gate. Come out on the grassy bank beside the river and commence your river walk by passing through another small wooden gate and along a bank with the lawns of a house on your left. Leave by a stile into pasture land and continue on with this on your left along the left bank of the river.

You are now on the Gipping Valley path and the way is clear and well sign-posted with stiles and bridges strategically placed along the way. You pass under the main Ipswich to Norwich railway line and, after nearly 1½ miles come out into a narrow country lane by Baylham Mill, which is said to have a medieval core. Turn left to walk up the lane towards the automatic crossing barriers at the railway track. Do not cross the line but turn right(SP) to carry on along a path bordered by fencing between the track on the left and a cultivated field on the right. You walk through a rather wet section before the path bears right to lead you back to the river. Carry on along the river path passing the attractively named Pipp's Ford, a timber-framed house away over on the right and later Bosmere Hall. A lake forms a conservation area with fishing rights on the left and here you come out on the road by a bridge.

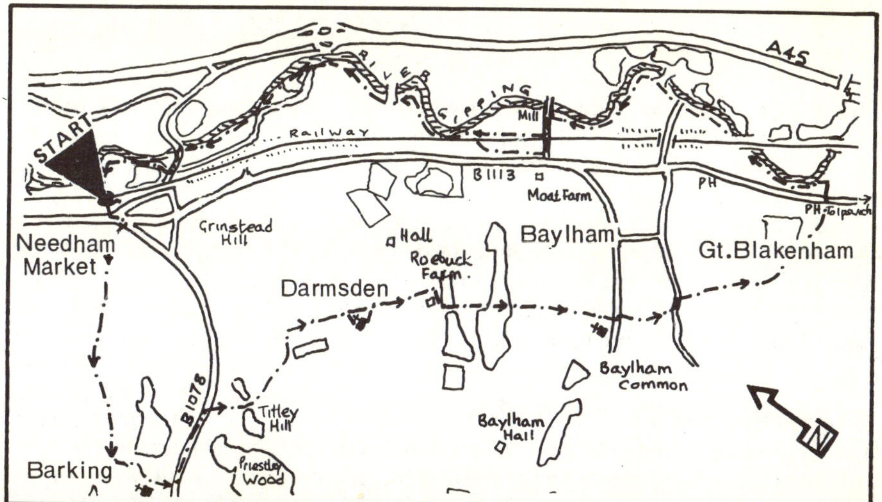

Do not cross the bridge but turn left and walk along the road passing Bosmere Mill on the right, now a restaurant. Pass the car park, go over the bridge and, at another car park by Bosmere Lake, turn off the road and walk across the grass. Carry on passing the lake on your left along a well-defined path across the meadowland. This is now a recreation area with seats and often refreshments. The lake is used by windsurfers who make a colourful picture, while for more serious purposes, police frogmen are trained in the waters. Continue for some distance past the end of the lake and when level with Needham Market railway station turn left along another path towards it. At the end of the park near the station turn right and walk a few yards until you are in line with the end of the signal box; here you will discover a tunnel leading you under the railway. Pass through the tunnel and across the station forecourt back to the car park and your starting point.

NUMBER TWO - RIVER GIPPING

Place visited: *Sproughton, Little Blakenham, Bramford.*
Distance: *7½ miles*
Starting Point: *Sproughton Church.*
Refreshments: *Sproughton Wild Man; Pubs in Bramford village.*
Map Ref: *1:25000 Pathfinder TMO4/14 1:50000 Landranger Sheet 155.*

SPROUGHTON MILL

THE WALK: Park in Sproughton village near the church and walk back up the street to meet the busy A1100 opposite the Wild Man public house. Turn right and walk along the footpath for about 400 yards until, just past the Bramford boundary sign, you turn left up 'The Grindle' a No Through Road. Just past Grindle Farm the track, now unmetalled, bears right. Another 500 yards sees you to Thornbush Hall where you go onto the concrete area and skirt to the left of the farm buildings. Continue on in the same direction as before and when a track crosses your path, take it left. After about 175 yards, and half way to Fidgeon's Farm ahead, turn right and head straight over the cultivated field to meet a country road.

Turn left and walk for about ½ mile along this quiet road. When the wooded area on your right ends, turn off the road and walk up the right side of the field with the narrow wood continuing on your right. The boundary of the wood sweeps left; when it then bears right, stop. Turn left and head across the open field in the general direction of the farm buildings beyond. The official right of way is towards Bullenhall Farm house to the right of the buildings but this involves going straight through the gardens just behind the house and the owner prefers you to cross the field and locate a track behind, and to the left of the farm buildings. Turn right onto this track (where it bears left is the point at which you would normally have joined it after walking through the garden).

The way soon leads you out into a narrow country road opposite Nubian Cottage. Turn right and after a very short distance go over the wooden farm gate on the left opposite the entrance drive to Tye Farm. Take the wide grass path beside the field on your right and at the end of the field turn right and follow the field boundary with a hedge on your left on the line of the telegraph wires. You join a track at the end of the field by a property hidden by trees and hedges. Carry on to the left of this for a few yards further and when the track opens out into a wide hardstanding, turn left to head down the right side of a cultivated field. Many field boundaries have been removed here giving the impression of open prairie. Go left and right to follow the boundary hedge and at the bottom bear right and walk down to the corner. Go through into a small field where you turn half right and head across to the far hedge to locate a farm gate. Cross over into a long narrow meadow. Turn right and walk to the end and on through the next meadow. At the end of this do not join the track by the farm buildings but go over the gate on the left just before the end of the meadow. Walk beside the buildings on your right to another gate. Turn right over this to pick up a drive which will lead you past the farm buildings of Little Blakenham Hall on your right and the garage block and hall itself set back over on your left.

Continue on leaving the farm and bearing left, then right at a cross drive. The drive then turns sharp left and you descend to the road by the village; the pits being worked over in the distance on your right provide chalk for the Claydon cement works, the hill itself is intriguingly known as Blood Hill. When you reach the road turn right and continue past the junction.

At The Beeches, a small development of modern houses, turn left. Continue past the properties on your left and follow a metalled lane right skirting a small grove. There are fine views over to the right as you climb and bear left. Half way past Coney Grove on the left go over a stile in a wire fence on your right and cross the meadow. Go over another stile in the far hedge where you are faced by a cultivated field. Keep straight on over the field parallel with the wood on your left towards a rough track ending abruptly on the far side. Join the track and head on down to the buildings of Broomvale Farm. Continuing past the farm reach the busy A1100 on a stretch of duel carriageway not far from its junction with the modern A45.

Cross both lanes with care and drop down to the service road on the far side. Turn left and walk past the properties bordering the road. Immediately past a pair of pinkwashed cottages go over a stile beside a metal farm gate(SP) leading down a track to another metal gate. Walk across to the railway track and cross it with care by means of two stiles; this is the main Liverpool Street to Norwich line. Enter a pasture and turn half right to head on through to the next, passing between two

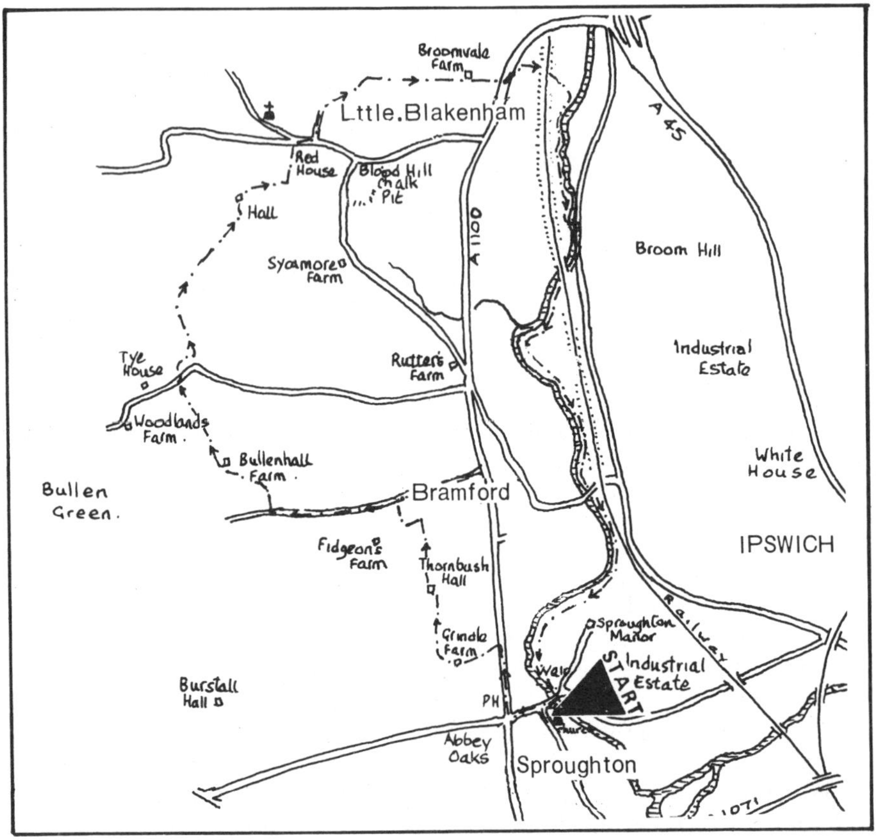

upright wooden posts. Follow the meandering cattle path which slowly closes on the river bank over to the left. Join the Gipping and continue along the right bank.

When you arrive at a mill and lock gates cross over the bridge to Paper Mill Lane a narrow country road. Turn right and walk for a few yards before taking a path right(SP) going behind the factory building to continue on a grassy path now on the left bank of the river. Go under the railway bridge and, later, pass a large housing estate on your right at Bramford. When the road bridge appears ahead you bear left away from the river to climb the steps to the road.

Cross the road and go down the other side(SP) to carry on through a recreation area beside the river. Go over a stile and footbridge and head towards Hazel Wood. This area is one of the most delightful on the Gipping walk as it continues on a woodland path beside the river then out into an area of rough ground beside a cultivated field. The Gipping which made a sweeping turn to the right at the wood now bears left and enters another wooded area. Passing the lock gates where the river drops some 8' to 10', and Sproughton Mill, you reach Sproughton Bridge where your walk terminates. Climb to the road and head back into the village and your starting point.

RIVER ORWELL

Orwell, delightful stream, whose waters flow
Fring'd with luxuriant beauty to the main!
Amid thy woodlands taught, the Muse could fain,
On thee, her grateful eulogy bestow.
Smooth and majestic though thy current glide,
And bustling commerce plough thy liquid plain;
Tho' grac'd with loveliness thy verdant side,
While all around enchantment seems to reign.

(I.I. Shewll)

NUMBER THREE - RIVER ORWELL

Places visited: *Trimley St Mary, Levington.*
Distance: *10 miles*
Starting Point: *By Trimley St Mary church off old A45.*
Refreshments: *Levington Ship; Pubs in Trimley High Road.*
Map Ref: *1:25000 Pathfinder TM23/33 1:50000 Landranger Sheet 169.*

LEVINGTON MARINA

THE WALK: Park by the churchyard wall in the 'No Through Road' by Trimley St Mary church. Walk out of the lane and cross the road. Turn left and, after about 200 yards, take the bridleway to the right by high trimmed hedges signposted 'River Orwell 1½ miles'. Carefully cross the railway track and continue now along a grassy path. At a crossways of paths turn left. Do not turn right to follow the footpath sign at the end of the field on your right, but instead carry straight on to meet a stony track. Turn right onto this and continue past houses to a metalled drive. Turn right towards the farm and outbuildings and then bear right onto a wide metalled avenue(SP) bordered by young and established oak trees. As you walk on, the massive cranes of Felixstowe container port are sighted just to the left of a straight ahead while, to the right, you catch glimpses of the Orwell. Continue on downhill for the best part of one mile to meet the river wall.

Turn right onto the raised grassy banks and commence a walk of over 2 miles round the Trimley Marshes, now reclaimed from the river and under crop. You can now look back to Felixstowe dock and, across the river, Harwich dock on the Orwell/Stour Estuary and Shotley Point on the Suffolk side.

When the bank ends, go down to the wide grassy track running parallel on the right and continue on this as it becomes a dirt track heading between high hedges. The track descends and goes off right. You continue ahead over a stile to walk a causeway between water and mud flats on the left and what appears to be a lake with many wild fowl on the right. Bear right with this well-worn path continuing along the side of the inlet from the river which mostly comprises mud flats. At the end turn left and drop down to the level of the marsh to head towards the trees; this area is a little sticky but the path well-defined. Enter the trees and climb a pleasant woodland path rising above Levington Marina on the left. The path then forks left and drops down to the Marina car park.

Walk on through the marina passing a lightship moored alongside the quay amidst the multicoloured yachts and small boats. Pass a private concrete road giving access to the marina coming down from the right and on past sailing equipment shops. Past the last 'finger' of water the concrete surface becomes grass as you bear left to head back to the river.

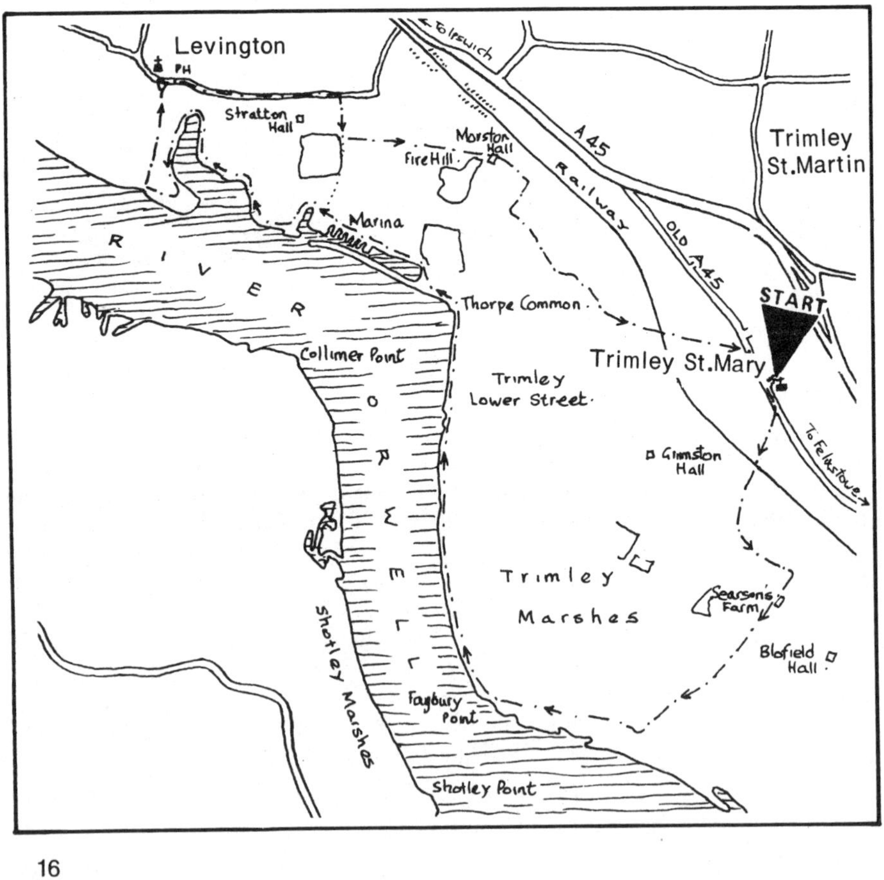

Climb the wall and continue on along the Orwell bank; part of the wall is new along this stretch and the land enclosed only recently reclaimed. The route curves inland and then, as you pass a dump, makes a firm right turn. The bank is now replaced by a track and you head away from the main river course on this. At the end go through metal gates, usually wide open, and turn almost back on yourself through a delapidated metal gate - do not go through the wooden gates of the Anglian Water Authority. Climb the bank which, for a few yards is very overgrown but then becomes a well-used path carrying you back to the river where you turn right.

When the river wall stops at a small 'beach' and you are confronted by trees and undergrowth, come down the bank on the right - the path follows this route - and head away from the river. Go through a cultivated field to meet the end of a hedge by a dead tree, at which point a footpath sign directs you up the field beside the hedge. Look ahead to the church at Levington and you may see your path outlined in the field heading just to the right of the church. Cross the stream ahead by a wooden footbridge and stile and continue up through a hay field, taking care to avoid two rather soggy sections encountered on the way. At the top(SP) take roughly the line of the church through a cultivated field where the path is usually well defined. At the end(SP) leave by a wooden gate and walk up a narrow path bordered by high hedging to come out into a country road opposite Levington Ship a public house with a history of smuggling and intrigue. Your route is right but there is time to visit St Peter's church a few yards to the left with its fine c16 red brick.

Turn right and then bear right with the road. You now face a ¾ mile long haul up the hill and past Stratton Hall before turning right down the concrete drive to Levington marina. When you draw level with the wood on your right, turn left and leave the road walking straight up the cultivated field. At the top pass to the right of a rather delapidated barn to pick up the end of a farm track. Go a few paces right and join a hedge bordering a field. Carry on with the hedge on your left and the field on the right down the hill. At the bottom you are confronted by Fire Hill a short stiff climb up the other side of the valley through heavy braken; there is a well-defined path under your feet though it is difficult to see through the undergrowth. At the top continue on along the left side of another field. The wood away over on your right turns to meet you as you join a track leading to the farm ahead by a pond. At the farm buildings, go between a hay storage barn on the left and an implement shed on the right. Bear left, over a stile and turn right to walk past Morston Hall.

When the drive is crossed by a track, turn right - left takes you over a railway crossing - and follow this track which goes left at a pillbox. When it leads into the grounds of a pair of cottages, skirt these to the right by a grassy path bordering a field on the right. Entering a wood the path becomes rather muddy as it wanders through the trees passing a strange and derelict Victorian building. You emerge to pass an elevated stretch of water on the left and go over a stile into a narrow metalled lane by some properties.

Go left and, ignoring the track carrying straight on with a footpath sign, follow the lane as it goes right. At the T junction go straight over along the left side of a narrow strip of field and to the right of a cottage garden. At the end of the garden stop and look across the open field ahead. Your way is roughly in line with the telegraph poles. On the other side, cross the road and go down the path opposite(SP) bordered by high hedges to the left of a pre-war bungalow.

Two stiles enable you to cross the railway track ahead and your path continues between cultivated fields. When a length of hedge starts, keep this on your left and at the end of the field on your right, go through it. Turn left and then right following the boundary of the next field and when the hedge ends turn half left and walk across the field on your left making a line for the bungalow which is six houses in from the roundabout on the main road - there should be a well-worn path here. When you come out on the road at Trimley, turn right and walk back along the road to the church and your starting point.

NUMBER FOUR - RIVER ORWELL

Places visited: *Wherstead, Freston, Chelmondiston, Pin Mill, Woolverstone.*
Distance: *14 Miles (Will split into shorter walks with starting points at both Freston Hill and Pin Mill).*
Starting Point: *Layby at bottom of Freston Hill on Shotley Road.*
(Short walks can be taken starting at Pin Mill car park, Chelmondiston).
Refreshments: *Butt & Oyster, Pin Mill; Boot, Freston; Pubs in Chelmondiston.*
Map Ref: *1:25000 Pathfinder TM23/33, TM03/13, TM04/14. 1:50000 Landranger Sheet 169.*

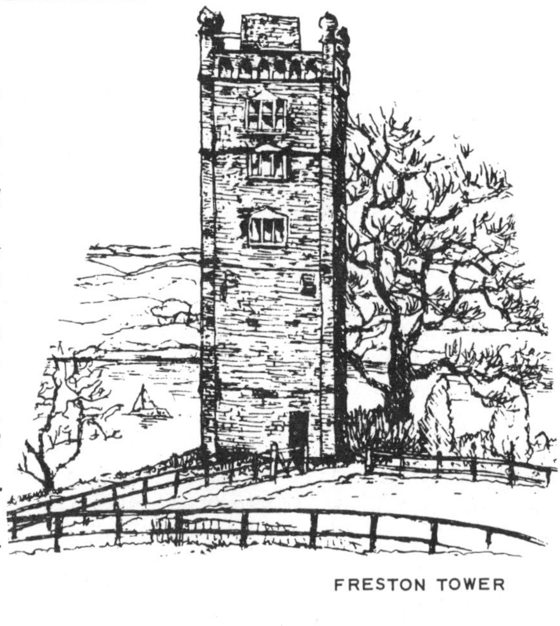

FRESTON TOWER

THE WALK: From the layby at the foot of Freston Hill on the B1456 Shotley road out of Ipswich, cross the road. Do not follow the footpath sign to Freston, but instead go through a gap in the hedge to the right of the sign into the corner of a cultivated field. Head diagonally across the field towards the right of Redgate Farm and its buildings. Cross Redgate Lane in front of the farm to enter the corner of another field.

Look across the field to where the Orwell Bridge meets the abutment and head for a point between the abutment and the first pier. Cross the concrete drive to Wherstead Hall by two stiles and continue across the meadow to the bridge. Pass the abutment on your left and the first pier on your right and continue on up the rise across the grass heading to the left of four pylons. Look ahead to the bungalows fronting The Strand and head down to the end of the line of fir trees bordering the rear garden of the first. Carry on behind the bungalows with a field on your left and after the last house go through a gap in the corner of the hedge along a path to the road.

Cross the Strand and take the footpath opposite signposted to the river. The path bears right to run parallel with the Orwell in the general direction of the Bridge to pass through Fox's boatyard. When level with the office, bear left(SP) to pick up the river path. Pass under the Orwell Bridge again bearing right to meet the road. Turn right and head in the direction of Ipswich for a few yards and take a wide concrete drive away from the river just before the cottage on the left.

Pass the point where you earlier crossed by the two stiles and continue on up the hill passing the church of St Mary with its Norman south doorway and then the offices of the Eastern Electricity Board at Wherstead Hall on your right. This late c18 mansion with a park designed by Repton was the home of the FitzGerald family between 1825 and 1835 during which period the writer Edward FitzGerald translated the 'Omar Khayyam'. Part of the Hall and its stable block was used as a convalescent home for soldiers during the First World War; the Board have been in residence since 1948. Pass the fine holly hedge bordering the grounds and meet the road on a bend.

Turn left and carry on past Park Farm. When the road bends sharp left, carry straight on along a private concrete farm drive. Reach the wood ahead and pass between the buildings of Wherstead Valley Farm and the farmhouse to meet a track. Turn left, and, just past the house, fork right along another track. On arriving at Cutler's Wood do not take the path left into the wood or the one skirting the wood to the right but continue on ahead through the edge of the trees. The path, at first a little concealed and overgrown, soon opens out into a delightful woodland track. When you emerge from the trees bear left and right with the path to carry straight on first with a barbed wire fence on the left, then between open cultivated fields. At the line of trees ahead, take the track left and when the trees end follow it with fields either side as it goes right and left towards Potash Farm. Pass the farm buildings and house on your right to reach the B1080 road just outside Holbrook.

Turn right and walk towards the village. After 600 yards take the drive going left signposted to Freston Grove near the speed limit sign. As you approach the farmhouse ignore the path going right and another coming in from the left. Turn right at the end of the garden boundary to pass white railings and head for a farm gate and post and rail fencing, keeping the farm buildings on your left. Go over the gate and along a narrow meadow leaving by another metal gate to descend another meadow to another farm gate at the bottom - ignore the track going right from another gate. Go over the gate into a cultivated field. Your way is straight up the field on a general line with the telegraph poles. Top the rise and continue to the end of the field opposite the house and buildings of Whitehouse Farm. Arrive at a junction of country lanes.

Go straight over and head for Woolverstone which you reach in ½ mile at the B1456 opposite the drive to Woolverstone Hall School; take this drive signposted 'To the Church'. Turn left in front of the church of St Michael, medieval in origin, but completely restored in 1889. Just past the church turn right and head across the park converging on the drive down to the marina of Harwich Yacht Club away on your left. When you meet the drive on the left side of the park, join it and continue down through the marina passing a car park and boat park on your right. At the end of the large building on the left, take a well-trodden path going east parallel to the river towards the trees.

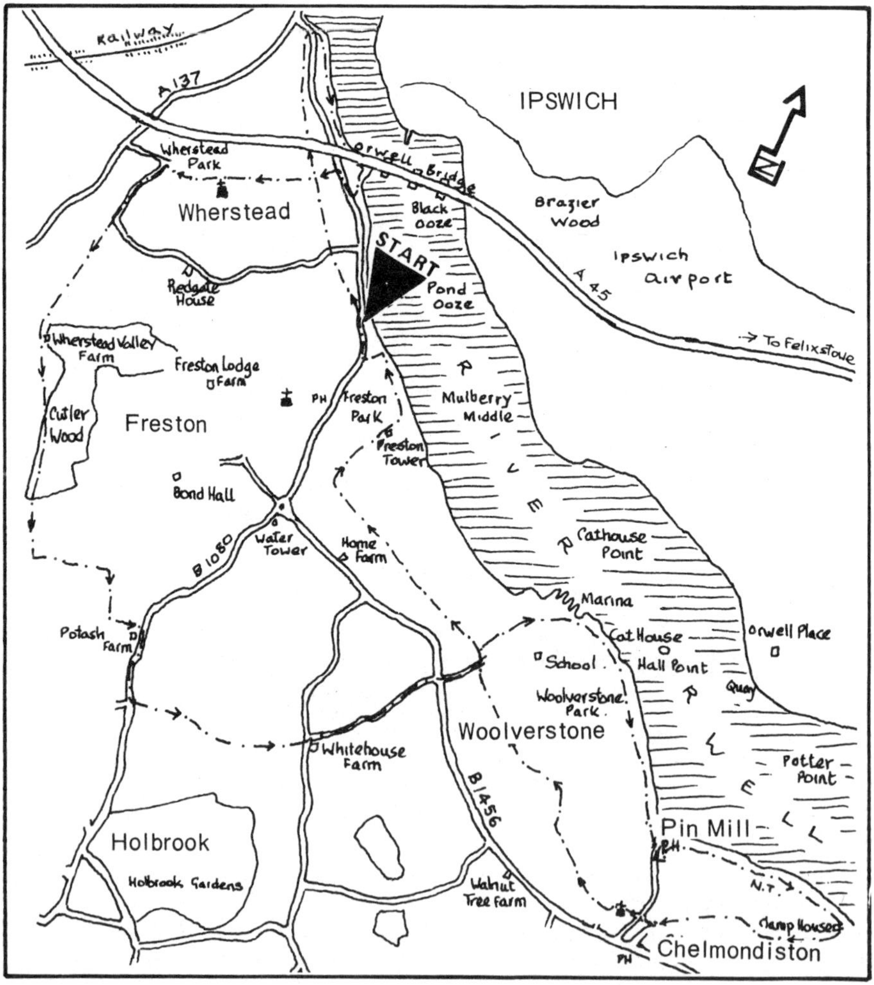

Walk this picturesque woodland path with, over on your right, Woolverstone Hall built in 1776 by William Berners, now part of a Greater London Council boarding school and, just north of the Hall by the jetty, The Cat House a Gothic-style building of 1793; its name derives from the days of smuggling along the Orwell when a white china cat was placed in a lighted window here if a run was on, to signify the coast was clear.

After about ½ mile another well-used path comes in from the right at an angle to join you. Continue for a further ½ mile with fine views before arriving on a narrow lane just to the right of the delighful Butt & Oyster Inn on the waterfront with a history going back to the c16 - just the place for a small detour and refreshments!

For the less energetic this is an ideal point at which to shorten your existing walk or commence another of less testing mileage. For the more intrepid, head back from the Inn, past the Pin Mill car park, and climb a set of concrete steps set in the bank on the left side of the lane. Pass between modern bungalows, along a short stretch of grass path to a cultivated field. Turn left to skirt the field and right at the end to pick up a path running parallel with the river. At first the path follows the edge of the field but later enters the trees to become a really rewarding walk with glimpses of the river below on the left; it is reassuring to note that the area is now under the protection of the National Trust. After about ¾ mile emerge, reluctantly, onto the lawns of Clamp House, a site going back to Doomsday Book when it was known as 'Pringles'; peat was stacked on the Hard here for the barges on their return passage to London.

Pick up a firm track right, away from the house and river. Bear right passing a man-made lake and continue on for some way to reach a group of farm buildings. Pass to the left of these and, ignoring the lane going left to the road, carry on a short distance to meet the lane down to Pin Mill.

Cross straight over up a lane winding its way left and right past St Andrew's church, totally destroyed in the Second World War and rebuilt with little imagination in 1957. Turn left at the top of the hill and right into Collimer Close, a small development. When the road bears right carry straight on along a wide cinder path. Cross over the next road and enter a dirt track passing a playing field on the right and after the last bungalow on the left continue on along a well-worn path beside the field.

You meet a firm track bordered by high hedges leading from the main road to your left and turn right onto this. When it forks, bear left signposted 'Bridleway to Woolverstone'. Follow the track until it turns sharp left to head for the road, at which point you leave it by going over the culvert on your right into a field and turning left to follow the left hand hedge in the same direction as before with cultivated fields on your right. Carry on with the main road running parallel one field over on your left until confronted by a large oak tree across the path.

At this point the path turns half right to run diagonally across the field. At the end carry on through rough ground, the path wandering down a dip then bearing left as it climbs to meet buildings on the edge of Woolverstone Hall School grounds. Go over a stile passing to the left of the buildings on a path bordered by wire and chainlink fencing. Bear left and right to a stile and enter a meadow which having crossed you leave by another to join the metalled drive to the school.

Turn right and head for the church again where you turn left. This time your route is straight on signposted to Freston. Cross the concrete drive to the marina and continue on a path beside the field. After some way you pass through a section of woodland and just past the entrance to Woolverstone House on the left, cross a metalled lane. Carry on to meet a metalled farm road on a bend and keep to this as it bears right and becomes a firm track.

Head for the woods ignoring a track which goes off left to the road and another going the same way as you reach the trees, you keep straight on passing to the right of the wood. Arriving at a farm gate, heed the instructions posted there and having entered the rough parkland make your way over to Freston Tower. This quaint folly was designed by William Latimer and built by Lord de Freston as a retreat for his daughter Ella's study around 1553. According to his instructions, the Lower Room was to be devoted to Charity from 7 in the morning until 8, the Second for working Tapestry from 9 until 10, the Third to Music from 10 'till noon, the Fourth for Painting from noon until 1, the Fifth to Literature 1 'till 2, and the Sixth, appropriately enough, to Astronomy in the evenings.

Carry on down to the foreshore and turn left to follow the river. Walk round a concrete wall structure and look for a shady path partially concealed in the hedge which leads you away from the waters through the trees to reach the road by a large layby. Turn right and walk down Freston Hill to reach your own layby and starting point.

NUMBER FIVE - ORWELL/STOUR ESTUARY

Places visited: *Shotley, Shotley Gate, Erwarton.*
Distance: *9 miles*
Starting Point: *Shotley Gate near the Bristol Arms.*
Refreshments: *Bristol Arms; shops at Shotley Gate.*
Map Ref: *1:25000 Pathfinder TM23/33 1:50000 Landranger Sheet 169.*

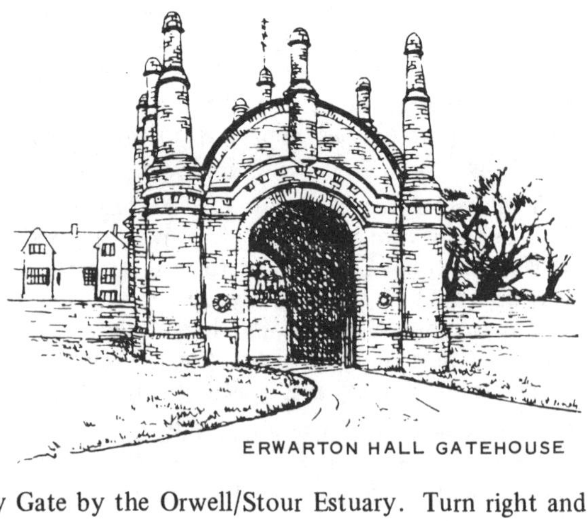

ERWARTON HALL GATEHOUSE

THE WALK: Park at Shotley Gate by the Orwell/Stour Estuary. Turn right and walk along the foreshore. After some way and after passing five natural wooden seats turn right by a fallen tree to climb away from the Stour with views across to Harwich and Parkeston. Climb steps up through the wood and follow the path as it meanders up and down to eventually meet the edge of the cliff.

Turn left to walk along the left side of a cultivated field with the river below you. At the end of the field pass to the left of a cottage and to the right of another. Head towards a double garage and pass between it and the house. Bear left and right to carry on as before along the field boundary. You pass mud flats on your left and, keeping with the path, climb the bank. Go over a brick bridge spanning a small stream and immediately right over a delapidated stile back to the edge of the field at a boundary.

Head straight up the right side of the field away from the river on a distinct path which soon becomes wide and grassy. In the trees look for a concealed footbridge over a ditch situated in a dip. Cross this and turn right then left to skirt a cultivated field. Carry on along the edge of the field towards the tower of Erwarton church. At the end of the field turn right up a dirt track between the gardens of properties. When level with the churchyard, now in a tree covered lane, turn left and head towards the church. Pass round to the left and enter on the far side.

This simple little church of St Mary with its beautiful views across to the river has associations with Anne Boleyn. Sir Philip Parker, her uncle, and his family are buried and have monuments here, while the heart of Anne, thought to have spent much time in Erwarton, is said to be contained in a casket now entombed beneath the organ. True or not, this church has a noticeable revered calm.

Go out of the church gate into the road and turn right. Continue on round the bend past the walled and terraced gardens of Erwarton Hall, built around 1575, to the extraordinary red-brick Jacobean gateway. This structure is undoubtably famed more as a folly than a work of art; it is roughly built and totally out of keeping with the hall.

Take the narrow country lane immediately opposite the gateway passing to the right of a pond. After passing cottages on your left the lane becomes an earthen track passing a wood on the left and another smaller one on the right. As you approach a house leave the track and skirt it going right and left along the field boundary. A track crosses your way and you turn right onto it walking between cultivated fields. At the end go a few steps right to carry on as before picking up a metalled lane which leads between farm buildings and cottages to the road.

Turn left and walk a few yards. Cross the road and the ditch by a small copse. Pass along the right side of the trees to the end. You are now confronted by an open field. Straight ahead is a farm, while just to the right and further away some farm buildings; head across the field in the general direction of the latter. You should reach the far side of the field in a corner. Carry on across the next to leave by a culvert into a narrow metalled lane.

Bear left and carry on - do not turn further left to descend the smaller track to a house. You pass cottages on your left and get a breathtaking first sight of the Orwell, usually crowded with yachts. Pass the farm and immediately before farm

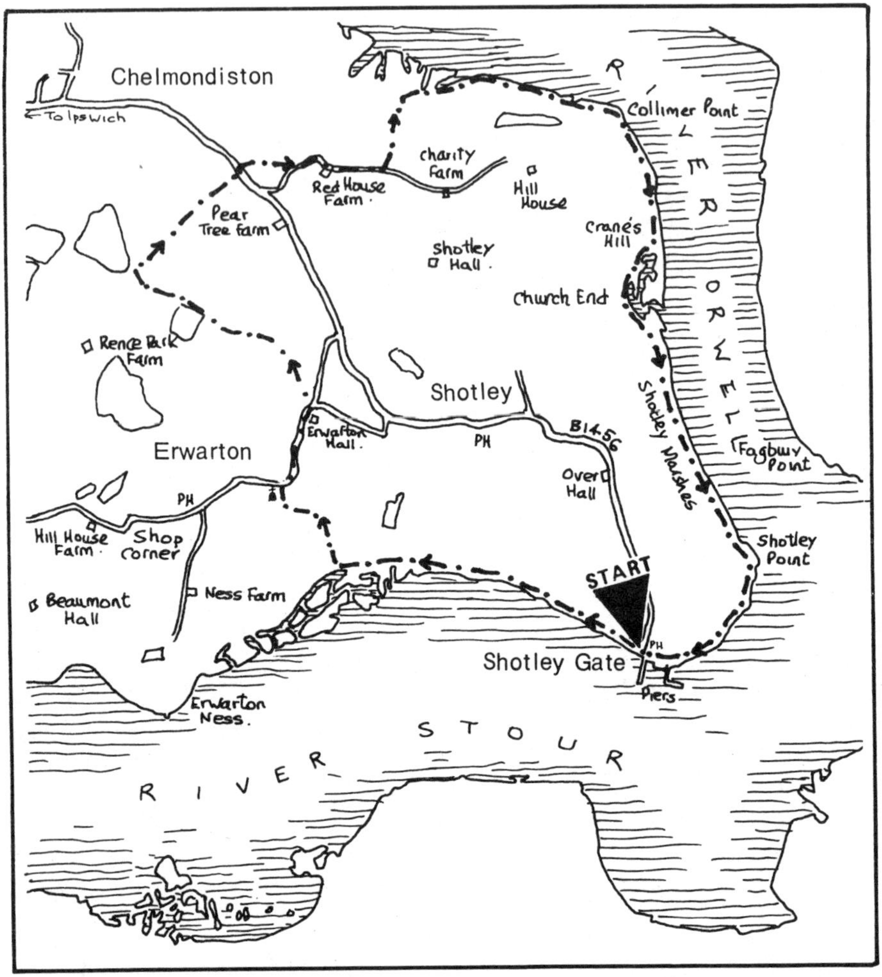

cottages on your left, turn down an earthen track. Bear right and then left at a house, then right again round the gardens. About 25 yards before a farm gate into a long narrow meadow, climb a rather faint path up the bank on your left and continue on above the river; when the tide is less than full you can clamber down the bank and walk along the foreshore.

A marshy inlet further along necessitates a detour round to the right and back again on your original line. Eventually you must climb the bank for the last time to walk the path which becomes well-trodden as you approach Shotley. The river wall becomes a concrete 'promenade' as you pass the old home of HMS Ganges over on your right, now the Eurosports Village, and walk on through the boatyard back to the Bristol Arms public house and your starting point.

RIVER STOUR

For Stour, a daintie flood, that duly doth divide
Fair Suffolke from this shire, upon her other side,
By Clare first coming in, and Sudbury doth show,
The even course she keepes; when farre she doth not flow,
But Breton a bright nymph, fresh succour to her brings:
Yet is she not so proud of her superfluous springs,
But Orwell comming in from Ipswitch thinkes that shee,
Shoud stand for it with Stour, and lastly they agree,
That since the Britans hence their first discoveries made,
And that into the east they first were taught to trade.
Besides, of all the roads, and havens of the east,
This harbour were they meet, is reckoned for the best.

(Michael Drayton)

NUMBER SIX - RIVER STOUR

Places visited: *Erwarton, Harkstead, Lower Holbrook.*
Distance: *8½ miles*
Starting Point: *Erwarton Church.*
Refreshments: *Queens Head, Erwarton. Bakers Arms, Harkstead.*
Map Ref: *1:25000 Pathfinder TM03/13, TM23/33. 1:50000 Landranger Sheet 169.*

THE STOUR NEAR HARKSTEAD

THE WALK: Leave the church on your left and walk along the road passing the small almshouses bequeathed to the parish by Sir Philip Parker; Boleyn Place, a small development of modern houses are on the right. The road bears left and after some 700 yards turn right off the road immediately past the Queens Head public house. After another 600 yards you meet a track coming in from the left and join it bearing slightly right of your previous route. Another ½ mile sees you to another junction of tracks at the end of a wood on your left. Turn left and pass the top of the wood on your left and then a small wood on your right. At the end of the trees your official route goes diagonally across the cultivated field on your right to the corner of the grounds of the property ahead, Crouch Cottage. As the owner prefers you to walk round the field, carry on along the track until you are level with the end of the field and turn right where the sign requests 'No Horses'. Keep the garden boundary on your left and, when it ends, turn left to follow the far boundary and meet a grassy path. Turn left and follow it back to the end of the track originally walked, so avoiding the section past the front of Crouch Cottage.

Carry straight on past a paddock on the right on a firm but unmade drive. Bear right and then take another track going left signposted to Rence Park Farm. As you approach to the right of farm buildings meet a crossways of tracks. Turn right and head in the general direction of Harkstead church in the distance. Pick up a metalled lane by some cottages which leads you out to the road on a bend. Carry on along the road and then take the left hand turning to the church as the road bears right. The church of St Mary is mainly c14 but has some Norman windows and a blocked Norman doorway; the tower has a splendid west window.

Immediately past the church go over a stile on the right (SP) by a letterbox built into the churchyard wall and walk along the right side of a meadow passing a pink cottage. Continue on through the next, and over a stile into a cultivated field. Carry straight on through the field a few yards in from the hedge and road on your right. Part of the way across the field you encounter a farm track and turn left to follow it down into a dip. At the bottom pass through a small meadow, over a metal gate, and up a rough track beside a field on your left. You pass to the left of Vale farmhouse and follow the boundary of the field left and right until you join the farm drive where you turn left and walk to meet a country road.

Turn right and after a short distance go through a gap in the hedge into the field on your left. Turn half right and head across the field on a line slightly to the left of the cottage on the far side. After 200 yards, stop, and turn left. Now head across the rest of the field to the far left hand corner. Go through the hedge and out onto a dirt track on a bend. Cross straight over the track and continue diagonally over the next field in roughly the same direction as before to the far left hand corner. Go through the hedge again to be confronted with another open field to cross. Head to the right of a clump of trees in the field and, beyond the trees, start to descend making for the end of the hedgeline on the right. Go through into the field on the right and walk along the boundary parallel with the road over on your left bordered by modern bungalows. At the elbow where the hedge ends continue on out into the field for a few yards before turning left to head down the remainder of the field roughly on a line with the radio mast on the horizon beyond the river. You should join the road through a wide gap in the hedge.

Turn right and pass Brook House on the left. Just past the semi-detached cottages River View and Bay View on the right, turn left down a wide cinder track signposted to the River Stour, Holbrook Mill and Stutton. When the track forks, bear left and when it goes down to the boats at the waters edge, bear left again along a well-worn path beside a field. At the river wall follow the path and the field boundary left. At a convenient spot go through the hedge and down the bank to the 'beach' and continue along the foreshore.

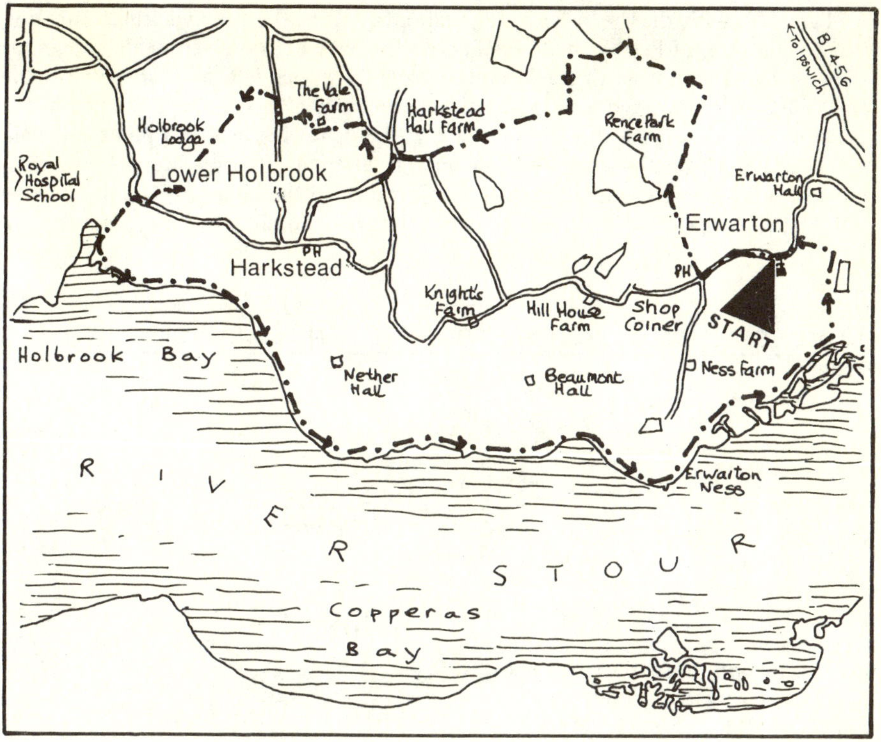

The walk along the shore is more pleasant than trying to continue along the field edge which is often overgrown and liable to subsidence.

You arrive at the river proper in Holbrook Bay and a further 1½ miles of enjoyable walking takes you to a position opposite Copperas Bay; Copperas was a material which looked similar to small pieces of twig, dug from the cliffs and used as a dye, colour wash for cottage exteriors and as an ink.

Further on you should be able to negotiate a section of mud flats and marsh but later you will be forced from the shore to the higher ground by more extensive marshes. Pick up the river wall and follow it round the inlet. When the wall ends, continue up the right side of the field. At the top keep along the field edge until you are again able to clamber down the cliff to the shore.

Walk round the point at Erwarton Ness and leave the beach for the last time by joining the river wall again at a point where a large drainage pipe runs out into the river from the shore. You are now being divided from the river by an ever increasing area of marsh and mud flats. When the bank becomes too overgrown, drop down to continue through the rough pasture on the left - many have been forced this way and a clearly defined path has been created. Carry on beside a field and eventually leave the line of the river at a point where you pick up a short length of wide grassy track at the end of the field.

Turn left with the green lane and head away from the river wall in a direction just to the right of Erwarton church ahead. The way becomes very wide and grassy then turns to a firm earth track approaching a man-made lake. Turn left off the track here going through a farm gate into a meadow. Walk up the right side of the meadow and look for a stile in the fence on the right. Leave at this point and walk up a path bordered by high hedging on the left and ferns on the right to cross another stile into the road. Turn left and return to the church and your starting point. (Some general information on St Mary's church is in Walk Number 5).

NUMBER SEVEN - RIVER STOUR/ALTON RESERVOUR

ALTON RESERVOUR

Places visited: *Tattingstone, Stutton.* **Distance**: *8 miles*
Starting Point: *Alton Reservour Car Park.*
Note - The gates giving access to this recreation area with its car park and toilets from Stutton are closed between 21.45 in the evening and 6.00 in the morning.
Refreshments: *Pub & shop in Stutton.*
Map Ref: *1:25000 Pathfinder TMO/13 1:50000 Landranger Sheet 169.*

THE WALK: From the car park and picnic area at Alton Reservour off the B1080 in Stutton, walk west along the grassy bank(SP). When you reach a seat turn left climbing a stile and taking a narrow country lane towards Stutton village.

You come out on the B1080 at an S bend where you turn left and almost immediately right by the Spar shop into Church Road. When the road becomes Lower Street on a left hand bend, turn right along a firm track(SP). The track becomes a well-worn path along the left side of a cultivated field with a hedge on the left. You meet a metalled country lane at a T junction and turn left. Pass Creeping Hall, Georgian, with a Venetian window. The removal of its original panes in the lower windows and their replacement with one large pane has somewhat detracted from its appearance.

Continue on a stony track by a large public footpath board to arrive at the river Stour by Stutton Ness and Doverhouse Point. Drop down to the beach here and look across Jacques Bay to Wrabness on the Essex side of the water and left across the estuary to the ships at Harwich.

Climb back up to the path and continue along the track with the river below on your left. Just prior to the end of the path, take another well-used path going down to the river again. Continue along the foreshore for about one mile noting the sandy cliffs with their strata of rock, such an unusual sight in this part of the country. Trees have fallen down the cliff as erosion has exposed their roots and you must make your way with care through the bleached branches. When the reeds completely block your progress work your way through them to a small clearing; do not continue further through the next area of reeds but climb the bank on your right.

Press on in the same direction along the top of the cliff and at the end of the field on your right, go through a wooded area to a large expanse of lawn bordered by a grassy bank. Keep on this mown bank and bear right as it sweeps round the inlet of the river heading for a large pink period house, Stutton Mill. Walk along the drive passing the house on your right and its outbuildings. Bear right and left with the drive as it becomes a metalled lane to pass the entrance to Queech Farm on the left (not seen from the lane). Bear right and left again and take a track off to the right. Ignore the first path going off left and after about ½ mile take the next leading to the B1080.

At the road turn left and, after about 200 yards, right into Upper Street. When the metalled lane ends continue on a track which bears left and then turn right. Shortly after it bears left again and then ends just past trees on the right. Look ahead to the farm buildings of Vale Farm and carry on in roughly the same direction. Bear right across the field as you approach the buildings to join a firm drive to the right of the buildings. Turn right and walk the ½ mile to the road.

Turn right and after ¾ mile, left. Another 400 yards or so sees you to the interesting folly known as the Tattingstone Wonder just beyond a left hand bend. About 1790 two cottages were given a new flint front with church windows and a third added in the form of mock flint church tower; as you see, the south side of the tower has no wall at all!

Cross the road from this quaint house to the start of the Alton Water Reservour walk by taking a public footpath by a stile(SP). Go over the stile and walk along a well worn path with the water away over on your left. The large impressive red-brick mansion is Tattingstone Place built in 1764. You reach a wood and continue on through the trees on a woodland path. At the end, the path bears left out of the trees and you pick up a grass path and continue with a cultivated field enclosed by a barbed wire fence on your right. At a footpath sign turn right to follow the field boundary and, at the next sign, left, to head down a dip and across an area of rough pasture to the next signpost sited on the rise by another cultivated field boundary fence. Keep this fence on your right and carry on as before along a meadow.

When you reach a small wood on the left by an inlet of the reservour, go over a stile on the right(SP). Walk through rough grass between the field boundary fence on the right and a bank on the left to the next footpath sign. Turn left keeping the field boundary fence on your right to another stile passing through an area

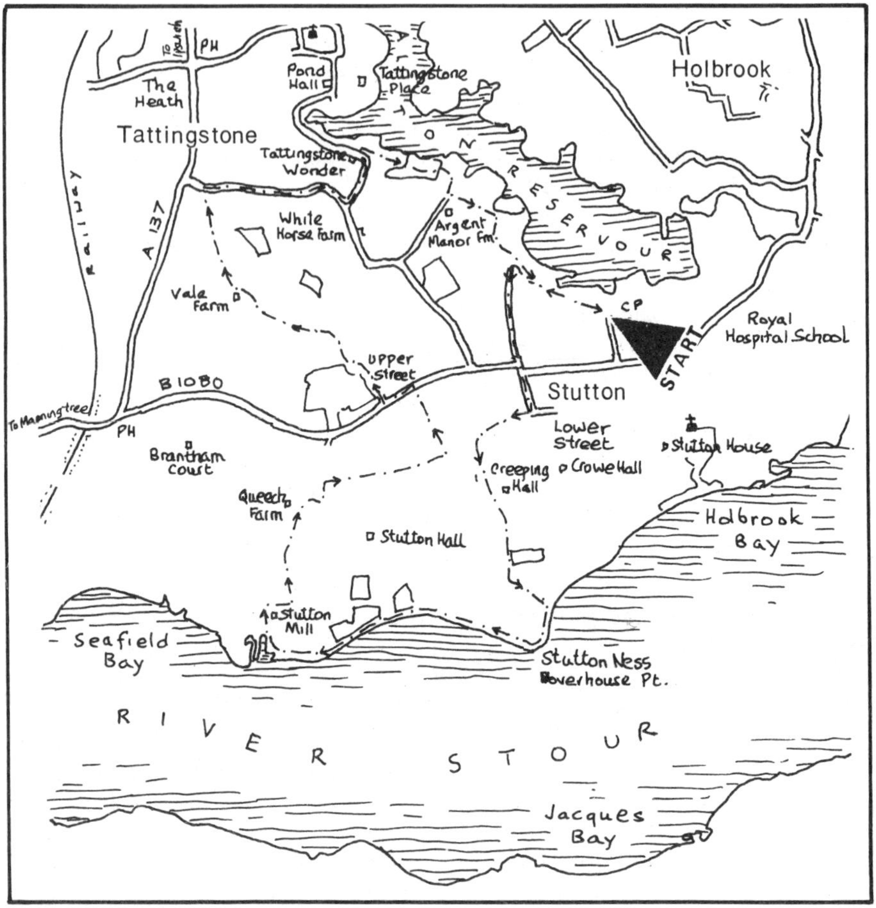

being landscaped with many young trees.

You now have superb views across the waters to the Royal Hospital School at Holbrook; there is a seat here overlooking the reservour.

The flooding of the Tattingstone valley to provide a water reservour for the ever expanding population of nearby Ipswich caused much controversy when it was implimented around the mid 70's, covering as it did valuable farmland, several properties and an area of much natural beauty. However, it has to be said that the lake created fits so naturally into the environment of this valley that few would now underestimate its recreational as well as commercial value. The Royal Hospital School beyond provides training for the sons of officers and men of the Royal Navy and Royal Marines. It was moved to its present site from Greenwich in 1933. The site is dominated by the clock tower.

This was the point at which you left the lake on the outward journey. Carry on straight ahead back to your starting point.

Places visited: *Stratford St Mary, Flatford, East Bergholt, Dedham (Essex).*
Distance: *5½ miles*
Starting Point: *Layby on Gun Hill (old A12) just outside Stratford St Mary.*
Refreshments: *Public Houses in Stratford St Mary; Restaurants and pubs in Dedham; Light refreshments available at Flatford Mill (summer).*
Map Ref: *1:25000 Pathfinder TM03/13 1:50000 Landranger Sheets 155/169.*

WILLY LOTT'S COTTAGE

THE WALK: Park in the layby half way down Dedham Gun Hill off the A12 just outside Stratford St Mary, and walk down past the house, along a metalled footpath, and out onto the road to pass The Tolbooth restaurant. Go over Stratford Bridge and turn right over a gate and stile(SP).

Go through a tunnel under the main road and turn left(SP) along a metalled track with the road above you on the left and a fence dividing you from a meadow on the right. Just past a crosshedge go over a stile set in the fence on the right(SP) into the meadow. Head to the right of the barn to reach a gate and bridge. Carry on through the next meadow with the river over on your right and cross a stile. Carry on to reach another stile to the B1029 road.

Turn left for a few yards and then right down a track to a stile, then follow the river bank for about 400 yards to a gateway in a vestigial fence. Now bear slightly left to walk the remainder of the meadow heading on a course leading you slowly away from the river bank to cross a gate set in the far hedge some 100 yards to the left of the river. Go over the gate to join a path fully enclosed by high hedges. At the end turn left along a wide lane. After about 100 yards cross Fen Bridge and in about another 60 yards go over a stile on the right. Follow a well-used path to a ditch and then head up the meadow towards the left hand corner of a wired enclosure; there are beautiful views over Constable's beloved Dedham Vale from here. Continue to a stile leading into a narrow country road.

Cross the road and a pair of stiles and walk diagonally over the field to another stile in the corner. Cross a track to yet another stile signposted 'Footpath'. Carry on through an area of rough grass planted with young and maturing fir trees, the faint path meandering downhill through long grass. The row of firs on your right screen a sewerage works but you may already be aware of its presence! You bear left to go through a gap in undergrowth to head uphill again along the edge of a copse on a firm path to a stile and gate opposite the drives to Clapper Farm and Clapper Farm House.

Turn right and walk along the road, narrow and usually quite busy in summer. After about 300 yards cross a stile on the left and follow the right side of the field beside the road. At the end turn left with the field boundary and, a short distance along the far hedge, turn right through a gap in the hedge(SP). After about 110 yards you will see an opening in the hedge on your right; go through this and turn left to walk down between high hedging on the left and fencing dividing you from a field on your right.

Reach the road and turn right to walk the short distance to the entrance at Flatford Mill. Visit the Mill and Willy Lott's Cottage, immortalised on canvas by John Constable who was born close by. Go over the bridge crossing the river Stour and turn right over the stile(SP).

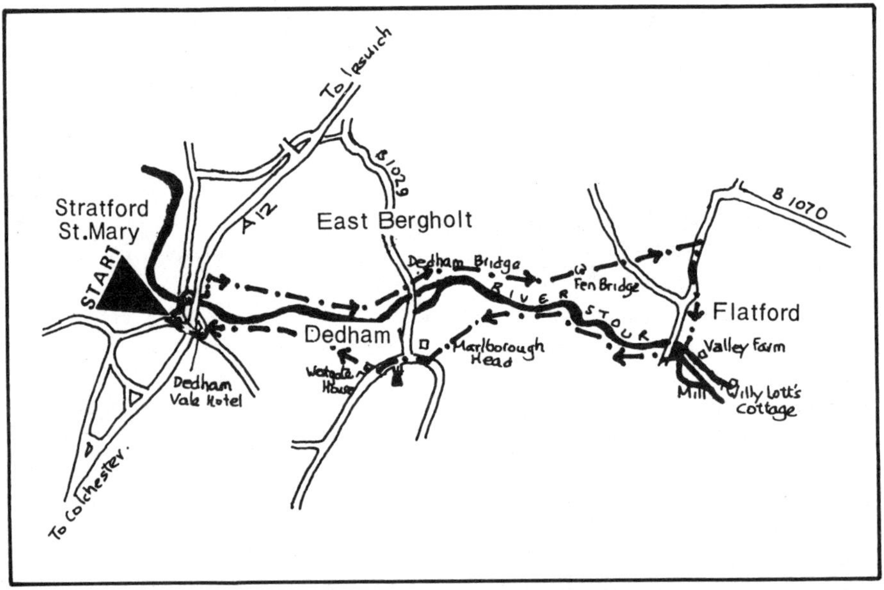

Walk along the left bank of the river for some distance until you reach a footbridge over the river with steel handrails spanning a wide dyke. Cross and bear half left to a white stile and a bridge and carry on to reach another white stile - the way is well defined and signposted as it leads you through a cultivated field. Continue with a copse on your right until a path bears right at another stile. Carry straight on to a gate and stile and then bear left of the farm buildings to a further stile and gate. Bear half right to reach the road via a gate in front of a cottage.

Turn right and walk into Dedham which, although in the neighbouring county of Essex, is an integral part of the Constable scene. Walk up the street past the impressive church on the left and just past Westgate House take the lane right to Bridges Farm which is under the National Trust.

FLATFORD MILL

Go through the farm buildings and continue on along a firm track with a hedge on your right to reach a gate and stile. On to another stile by the river then passing a copse on the left reach a kissing gate. Go through the wood past a house on your left and up the rise through the trees to emerge on the road opposite Dedham Vale Hotel. Turn left, then right over the bridge spanning the A12 and, almost immediately, right again to arrive at the metalled path beside the white fence which will lead you back to the layby and your starting point.

RIVER DEBEN

No stately villas, on thy side,
May be reflected in thy tide;
No lawn like parks, outstretching round,
The willing loiterer's footsteps bound
By woods, that cast their leafy shade,
Or deer that start across the glade;
No ruin'd abbey, grey with years,
Upon thy marge its pile uprears;
Nor crumbling castle, valour's hold,
Recalls the feudal days of old.

Nor dost thou need that such should be,
To make thee, Deben, dear to me:
Thou hast thy own befitting charms,
Of quiet heath and fertile farms,
With here and there a copse to fling
Its welcome shade, where wild birds sing;
Thy meads, for flocks and herds to graze;
Thy quays and docks, where seamen raise
Their anchor, and unfurl their sail
To woo and win the favouring gale.

(Bernard Barton)

NUMBER NINE - RIVER DEBEN/WOODBRIDGE

Places visited: *Woodbridge, Melton.*
Distance: *6½ miles*
Starting Point: *Wilford Bridge Picnic Site on the A1152 at Melton.*
Refreshments: *Ample in Woodbridge.*
Map Ref: *1:25000 Pathfinder TM25/35, TM24/34 1:50000 Landranger Sheets 169, 156.*

WOODBRIDGE TIDE MILL

THE WALK: From the car park at the picnic site head for the river wall. Climb the wall and turn left heading along a well-worn path towards Wilford Bridge. At the bridge join the busy B1084, cross over and bear slightly left to head down the metalled lane opposite. Cross the railway track and when the lane bears right to a property, carry on straight ahead along a wide green track. The way then turns left along a narrow but well-used path which heads towards the trees. The path becomes a firm dirt track as you pass the rear gardens of modern houses on the left and bears right through attractive woodland to meet the road.

Cross the B1438 and continue up the narrow lane opposite which turns right and then bears left to a junction. Turn left here and gradually descend a hill. When a lane goes left on a right hand bend, continue right and left for a further few yards to meet the road. Turn left and after a few yards, right by a group of tall trees along a rather overgrown cart track. The boundary of the wood on your left takes a loop left while you carry straight on over rough grass to pick up the edge of the trees again continuing along the left side of a cultivated field.

At the end of the field go through the barbed wire fence on the left in the corner and continue in the same direction as before through the wood which is almost head high in braken. There is no indication of the route to take here and you must just press on until you reach a ditch on the edge of the trees and cross, by a plank footbridge if your aim is right, to climb over a post and rail fence into an area of paddock. Head over the rough grass to a point just to the right of a stable block. Bear left here to negotiate two metal gates along a track which leads you out into a narrow metalled lane. Keep left to walk the short distance to the main road.

Go a few yards right then cross to head up Leek's Hill, a lane servicing a number of individually built detached houses attractively sited among the trees. When the lane goes right at Leeks Hill House, carry straight on along a very pleasant woodland path(SP). Bear left and descend the hill arriving at the bottom to turn right on an unmade road. Turn right along a footpath by the notice board stating 'Private, no motorcycles' to skirt the properties on the right. The path bears left, bordered by high hedges on your right, and eventually comes out on a road which you cross to take an alleyway to the right of The Christian Servicemen's Centre.

Arrive in Sun Lane, turn right for a few yards, then left to walk up St John's Hill. Press on ahead down a road fronted by 'No Entry' signs. At the end turn right and continue to thread your way through Woodbridge passing the Mariner's Arms and then Ye Old Bell & Steelyard arriving at The Bull Hotel on the corner of the Market Square. In the centre is the impressive Shire Hall built by Thomas Seckford in 1570. The lower part was, until 1803, open and stood on supporting pillars to provide a covered market.

Bear left passing St Mary's church on your right with its fine 108' tower decorated with flushwork and head down Church Street. Half way down turn right into Turn Lane which narrows to an alley between properties before emerging on one of the main roads leading into the town centre. Turn right and then go up a lane on the left between Old Malting House on the left and Half Moon House on the right. Cross straight over the next road into Kingston Road.

As you approach the recreation ground, skirt it to the right by turning into

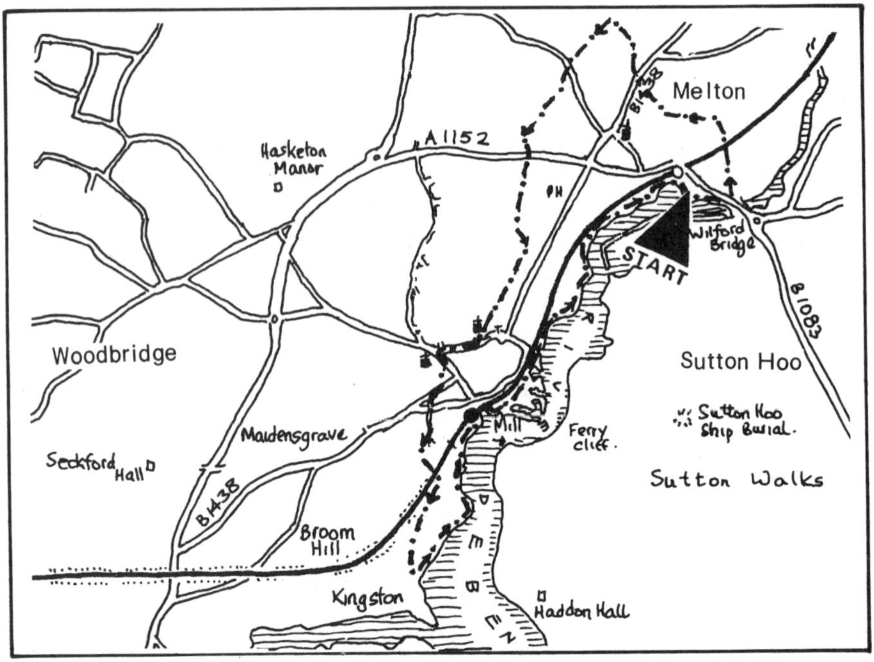

Kingston Farm Road and, at the end, go onto the shingle drive of the house and turn left along a dirt track with the hedge bordering the recreation ground on your left. Cross the railway track by stiles on either side and follow the path right running parallel to the railway lines. You now walk a well-trodden way through trees and meadows gradually bearing left to converge on the river wall.

Climb the bank and turn left, the metalled path with an occasional seat providing a civilized ¾ mile stroll by the Deben back to Woodbridge. At the point where the wall bears left look across the water to the fir trees forming a wood on the far hill; beyond the trees is the site of the world-famous Sutton Hoo burial mounds. The treasure ship discovered in one of the tumuli in 1939 had to be dragged up the hill from a point somewhere along the river bank. The boats become more numerous as you near town and you can clearly see the prominent outline of the Tide Mill ahead.

Walk the concrete promenade and pass through the buildings of the boatyard. You can visit the town or leave the route for refreshments by crossing the railway track at the level crossing gates.

Back on the route go right to visit the Tide Mill but the walk goes straight on(SP). There was a tide mill on this site as early as 1170, the present one is probably c17 and was working until 1956. The path bears left to a second set of level crossings; do not cross but continue with the track on your left until the path bears right to take you back to the river bank. Turn left and complete your walk with a pleasant saunter beside the Deben back to the picnic site and your starting point.

NUMBER TEN - RIVER DEBEN

Places visited: *Waldringfield.*
Distance: *4 miles*
Starting Point: *Public car park near The Maybush public house at Waldringfield.*
Refreshments: *Maybush Inn, Waldringfield.*
Map Ref: *1:25000 Pathfinder TM24/34 1:50000 Landranger Sheet 169.*

WALDRINGFIELD

THE WALK: From the car park walk down to the road by the Maybush public house and turn left. Take the first turning right and after just over 600 yards turn right down a track, ignoring the 'Private' track going straight on and the road turning left. Bear left and then turn right to a boathouse set in the trees where the track ends. Go through the trees along a narrow but well-used path(SP). It turns right by a cottage and takes a meandering course through braken towards the river.

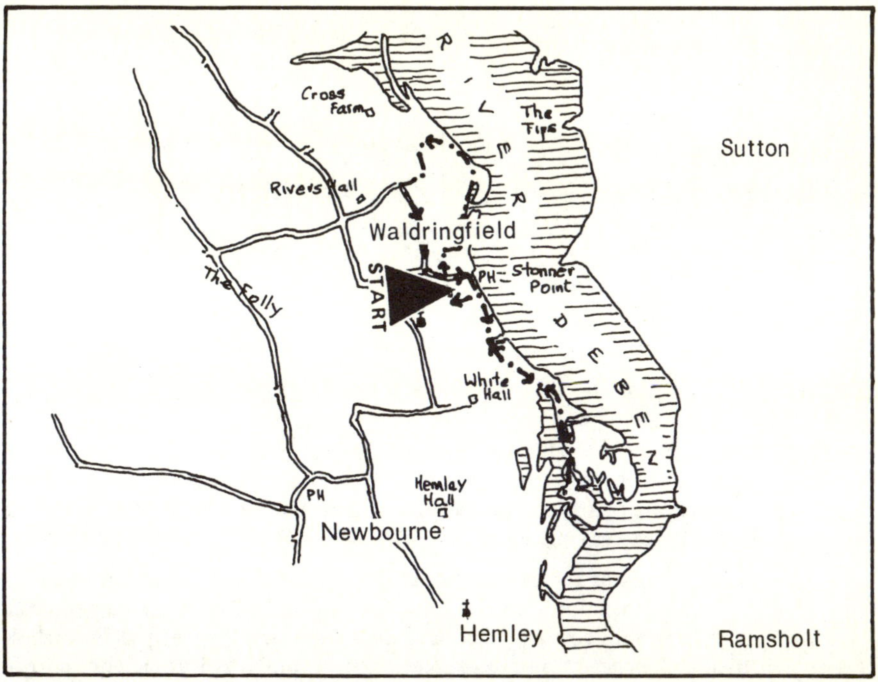

Bear right to pick up the river wall which although at first rather overgrown, soon develops a clear path. When you arrive back in the centre of Waldringfield pass houses fronting the river and then turn right and then left to skirt the marina(SP).

Turn left at the road by the Maybush down to the quay where you turn right along the foreshore. Skirt to the right of a boat park by beachhuts before continuing along the river wall then bearing left to pick up a path running by the left side of a cultivated field. Later the path bears left over a grassy area to join the river wall which then forms a causeway leading out into the Deben.

Continue on this narrow strip of land with water on either side. The walk here is exhilarating but beware of the tides as the path drops in places almost to water level even at low tide and will certainly be difficult to negotiate at high tide. It is best to turn back after no more than ½ mile and retrace your steps.

After repassing the boat park and the beachhuts you will see concrete steps climbing steeply up from the shore. Take these leading you back up to the pub car park. Continue on through to the public car park and your starting point.

NUMBER ELEVEN - RIVER DEBEN

Places visited: *Felixstowe, Falkenham.*
Distance: *9 miles*
Starting Point: *Car Park by the cafe at Felixstowe Ferry.*
Refreshments: *Felixstowe Ferry pub and cafe.*
Map Ref: *1:25000 Pathfinder TM23/33, TM24/34 1:50000 Landranger Sheet 169.*

FELIXSTOWE FERRY

THE WALK: From the car park pick up the river wall path which runs from the road bordering the golf links. The path has a metalled surface at first as it runs along the south side of a small creek then heads west passing the golf links on the left; the large building across the estuary at Bawdsey is Bawdsey Manor built in 1886. A car-ferry used to cross the Deben between Felixstowe and Bawdsey here by means of a chain and steam engine.

Follow the left bank of the Deben and, after about 700 yards, bear left and then right near the small wind pump to skirt the King's Fleet, a drainage channel which flows across the marshes to the Deben and discharges near the ferry. This whole lower part of the Deben was once the great open port of Goseford, a wool port of the Saxons and where Edward III assembled his fleet for the Calais expedition.

Turn north-west with the wall again and continue for a further 1½ miles before skirting Falkenham Creek. Continue on as before noting the ancient round tower of Ramsholt church across the water; probably once used by the Saxons as a watch tower against Danish invasion - from the top there are views along the whole length of the Deben from Woodbridge to the sea.

After another mile or so bear left away from the river at Kirton Creek, once Guston, a busy customs port with ferries linking with Ramsholt and Shottisham. Head inland and, when the water ends, come down the river wall and cross into a meadow by a stile over a barbed wire fence. Turn right and walk along the right side of the meadow to leave at the end by another stile onto a firm farm track. Turn left and head up the rise to meet another. Turn right into this and pass a timber shed and then bear left towards the farm buildings of Kirton Lodge. When you reach the concrete drive by the buildings turn right and walk between a new steel barn on the left and an implement shed on the right. Continue on until you reach a cross roads; straight ahead and right are unmade, you go left onto a metalled road.

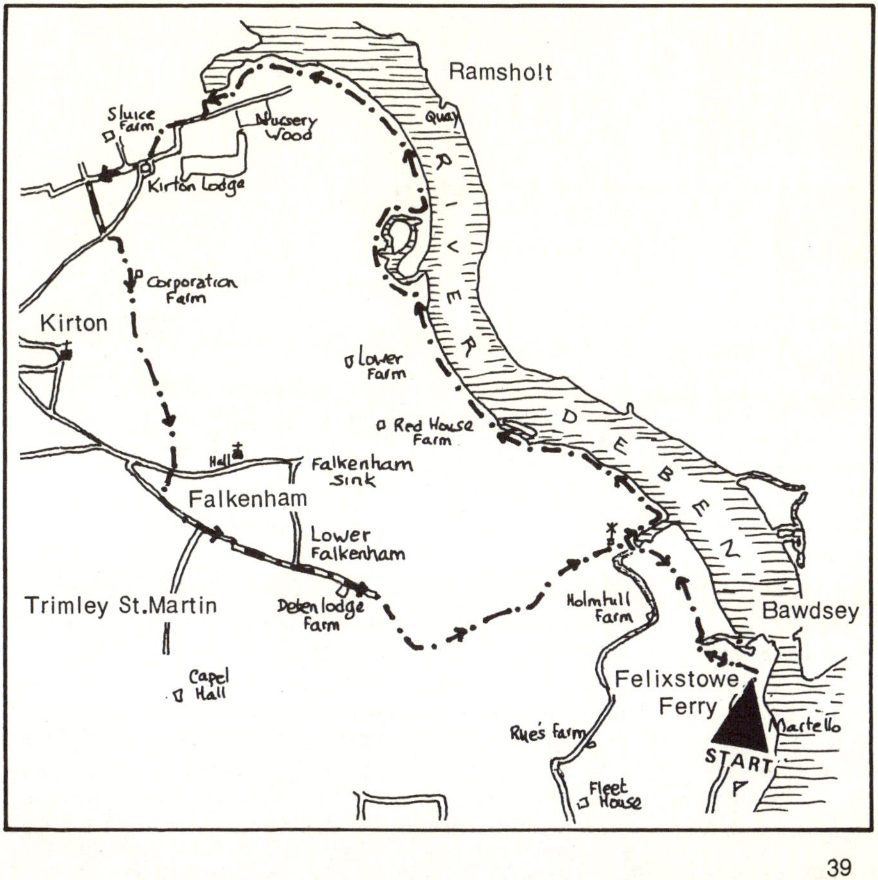

When you come to a sharp right hand bend, turn left along another concrete drive passing to the right of the Lodge bungalow. Bear right with the drive and then bear right along a bridleway(SP) immediately before the first farm building on the right at Corporation Farm.

You pick up a track and continue for some way on a variety of surfaces, hoggin, concrete as it drops down a dip, then, as it climbs again, a dirt track and finally green lane before it comes out onto a small country road opposite a white gate. Cross the road and go over the gate(SP) and walk along the shingle drive beside the house. Leave the grounds by crossing over another wooden gate onto a track. Follow this a short distance ahead to join another quiet country road.

Turn left, walk past a right turn, then a left turn to Kirton. At Deben Lodge Farm the road becomes a track and you carry on past the 'Private Road' sign. When the track bears left you are again joined by the King's Fleet on your right and after nearly one mile meet the river wall again near the wind pump you passed on the outward journey. Climb the bank and turn right to retrace your steps back to the ferry and your starting point.

The Ferry Boat Inn stands on a very ancient site with records of a Ferry House as far back as 1181. In the 15c the present building became a Fish Mart where fish caught in the Deben and adjacent waters were sold.

NUMBER TWELVE - RIVER DEBEN

Places visited: *Shottisham, Sutton, Ramsholt.*
Distance: *10½ miles*
Starting Point: *Shottisham Church.*
Refreshments: *Pub, Shottisham; Ramsholt Arms.*
Map Ref: *1:25000 Pathfinder TM24/34 1:50000 Landranger Sheet 169.*

RAMSHOLT

THE WALK: Leave the church on your right and walk along a narrow metalled lane going down past cottages on your left. When the lane turns right go up the left side of Tudor Cottage and turn left into a green lane overhung by high hedging, bearing right into a field when your way ahead is blocked. Continue along the left side of the field and out through the corner into a meadow. Turn half right and head diagonally, over a depression, to cross a stream by a substantial brick bridge. Cross the adjacent barbed wire fence, the stile usually sited here is missing. Turn half left and continue through the remainder of the meadow towards a red brick cottage where you leave the meadow by a stile into the road.

Go straight over and up the metalled lane towards Wood Hall Hotel. Carry on past the entrance and at the fork by the thatched Sutton Hall office building bear right. When you reach the entrance to Sutton Hall on the right go left along a firm track which passes the gamekeeper's cottage on the left.

At a crossways of tracks take that going right, a green lane bordered by overhanging hedges. When you break out do not bear right with the track but fork left along a grass path towards the left side of the wood ahead. At the trees pick up the track and turn left. Head between cultivated fields and at the end follow the track right. When the field on your right ends, just before the commencement of a line of fir trees, turn right with the track and head back along the top of the field. Half way back to the wood, a length of hedgerow commences, and just prior to this turn left on another track which heads away between two further open cultivated fields. The track continues up the rise, through a gap in the field boundary hedge then descends to join a quiet country road among trees.

Turn left, pass a pair of cottages on the left as the road bears right, and keep on for some ¾ mile to locate a footpath sign on the left. Leave the road and follow a grass track between fields climbing steadily. At the top pass through an opening and head diagonally down the next field to meet the river wall in the bottom right hand corner near a cottage.

Climb the grassy bank and turn left. This is the derelict quay of Methersgate, the landing place for the Manor of Campsea in the Middle Ages. You now commence a five mile walk along the banks of the Deben but if the tide is in it will prove very difficult to negotiate, particularly the first section to Stonner Point. There are some delightful little sandy beaches along the route, normally only accessible by boat, but the river wall is usually broken at these places and replaced with dense woodland and thick reeds which force you to skirt round the back via the field edge. The wall itself is also covered in long grass with no sign of a path and progress will be slow.

You pass one of the most enchanting spots on the river, The Tips; these sandy points were built out into the river during the latter part of the last century by Robert Knipe Cobbold, a Sutton farmer, in an effort to reclaim 150 acres of land. He intended to carry them even further out over the mud but Trinity House put a stop to the proceedings when it was feared that navigation and even the course of the river could be affected.

After 1½ miles of by far the most difficult going, you arrive at Stonner Point, once a manorial landing place called Woodhall Stonner where quite a large settlement formerly existed round the Green at the back of the Point. The Quay here was built by Thomas Waller of Sutton Hall about 1850 for the purpose of shipping coprolite - a fossalised animal dung dug up in large quantities all over the neighbourhood and used as a fertilizer. Thousands of tons were shipped annually from the Debenside quays to all parts of the Kingdom.

From here the going is easier and the way more defined; across the water are the boats moored at Waldringfield. You pass Shottisham Creek and then, on the other

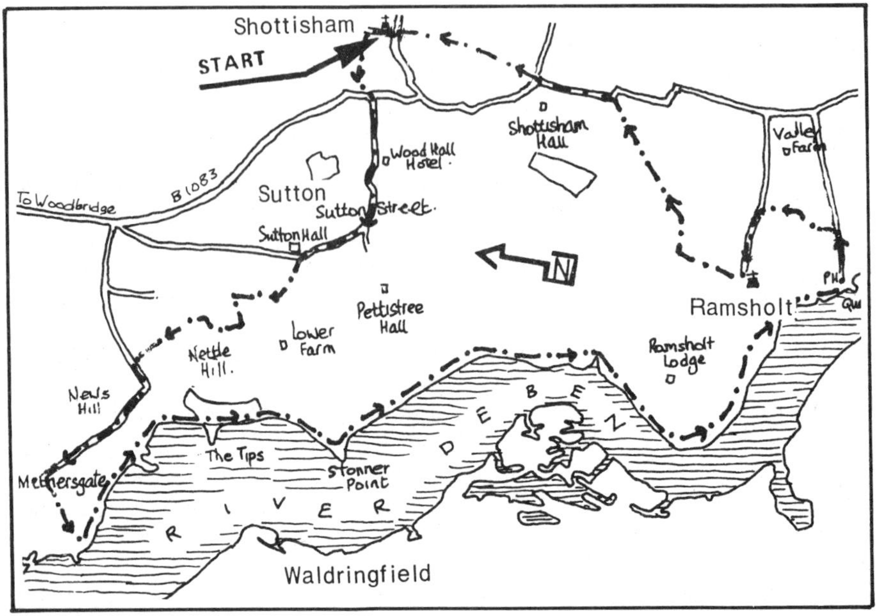

side of the water, Hemley where salt was manufactured in saltpans; the small creek and dock was constructed by Charles Cooper of Red House Farm towards the end of the last century.

When you approach Ramsholt, a clear path develops and the last half mile to the Ramsholt Arms public house is almost civilized. Leave the beach in front of the pub, once the ferry house for the crossing to Kirton, and walk up the road away from the river, passing the entrance gates and the large hotel sign. When you approach a house on the left after the car park, along this tree-lined road, turn left down a sandy track through the trees. Bear right at the bottom of the valley and pass round between two properties. Bear left at the back of the houses and continue up a stony track to reach a metalled lane. Bear left onto this and head to the church. All Saints has a Norman tower which, although it looks oval, is in fact round. It is believed to have Saxon origins and to have once been a lookout tower; a view of the whole length of the Deben from Woodbridge to the sea can be had from the summit.

Turn right from the church along a firm track and when you meet another turn right again. Bear left then continue on passing to the left of a small wood - do not take the fork right here. Over ½ mile further on you meet a road at a bend by an overgrown pillbox, turn left here. At the bottom of the hill cross straight over the B1083 and head up the sandy track opposite. When this turns right, carry straight on along a grassy track which becomes a green lane passing between high hedges to eventually come out on a metalled lane. Continue on heading down the hill to the village centre and pub. Left and right will return you to the church and your starting point.

RIVER WAVENEY

Listen to me -
There is a little river, fed by rills
That winds among the hills,
And turns and suns itself unceasingly,
And wanders through the cornfields wooingly,
For it has nothing else to do, but play
Along its cheery way:
Not like great rivers that in locks are bound,
On whom hard men doth heavy burdens lay,
And fret their waters into foam and spray.
This river's life is one long holiday
All the year round.

(Jean Ingelow)

NUMBER THIRTEEN - RIVER WAVENEY

Places visited: *Syleham, Weybread.*
Distance: *7½ miles*
Starting Point: *Pull in just before Syleham Bridge on the road from Brockdish village.*
Refreshments: *There are pubs in Brockdish, though none on the route.*
Map Ref: *1:25000 Pathfinder TM28/38, TM27/37 1:50000 Landranger Sheet 156.*

THE RIVER AT WEYBREAD

THE WALK: Proceed along the narrow country road the few yards to cross the bridge and lock over the River Waveney which divides the counties of Norfolk and Suffolk. This bridge, built in 1847, was until some years ago accompanied by a toll-gate, this being the only crossing of the river for some distance. Continue to the junction in the village of Syleham and turn left passing Syleham Mill, which now manufactures ready-made clothes but formerly made drabbets, smock-frocks made from a drab twilled linen, the machinery then using water power from the river. Just past the prefabricated building, turn right climbing steadily up a concrete track.

When this turns left towards Top Barn Farm, carry straight on up the right side of a cultivated field. At the top go into the next field by a culvert over the ditch. Cross this narrow field and turn left to walk along the top boundary with a ditch on your right. At the end bear left over an area of rough grass to leave by a culvert into a narrow metalled road on a bend.

Turn left and continue for about ¾ mile passing a turning to the left. The road takes a curve to the left and then bears right at a bend by the entrance gates to Syleham Hall. A short distance further on go over a metal farm gate on the left and head across the meadow to another on the far side. Go over this into a cultivated field, and keep straight on in line with the telegraph poles. Half way across the field start to bear right in a sweep to take you to the left of the garden of the cottage ahead. Pass on down to the road beside the tall clipped boundary hedge. Go over the ditch and turn left.

After a few yards go down the farm track on your right, past the farm buildings and over the metal gate into a meadow. Walk down the meadow beside the hedge and when it ends turn half left and go down the steep slope to arrive by the trees in the far left hand corner. Go through the barbed wire fence and make your way down through the trees with another wire fence on your left. Coming out into the valley bear left to follow the fence and negotiate another across your way. Turn right now and make your way over to the stream which you cross by a wooden footbridge. Make for an opening in the trees up the rise to join a cattle track to a substantial metal gate. Go over the gate and continue on ahead through the meadow and a gap in the far hedge. Do not bear left with the track to the buildings of Weybread Hall but keep straight on to locate a stile in the far hedge.

Come out onto a metalled lane and turn left towards Weybread. Pass a bungalow on the left and a cottage on the right near the Hall. Join a country road on a bend and carry straight on to the entrance gates to the delightful St Andrew's church, with its round Norman tower. Though it has been described as over-restored, I found little of the usual Victorian bad taste here.

Continue on round the right hand bend and eventually meet the B1116 Roman Road by the attractively sited village sign. Cross the road and head up the right side of a field just to the left of the bus shelter. Follow the field boundary to the end and carry on through the next field of fruit bushes. At the end you have ahead of you a man-made lake belonging to the farm on the right. You must skirt it by turning left then right over the ditch to continue along behind the grass bank created from the spoil. Go through the hedge ahead and bear left through the next field to emerge from the far left hand corner into a green lane.

Walk along the lane, first with a hedge on your right then between open fields. At the end turn left on a track immediately beyond the far hedge. When the track turns left, carry straight on with a hedge on your right. Continue on in the same direction through the fields and enter a meadow. At the end go through an opening in the hedgrow to carry on down the hill with old sections of hedging on your left towards a white thatch cottage with brick outbuildings to the left. At the bottom enter a narrow country lane through an opening in the hedge by a footpath sign, the first of only about three encountered on the whole walk!

Turn left and walk for a short way along this very rough metalled lane. Just before the white cottage on the right, climb the bank to walk along the right side of the vegetable garden away from the lane. When the garden boundary ends continue over the remainder of the meadow to the far hedge. Turn right and follow the hedge until you can find a convenient place to cross the barbed wire fence and enter an area of sand pits; the best place appears to be by a large single oak tree. Look straight over the workings to an exit gap and metal gates on the far side. Work your way with care skirting to the right of the pits ahead to reach the road by this gateway.

Turn left and after a few yards left again at a road junction; the lake on the right is used for windsurfing. Continue along this quiet road passing another stretch of water on your right to reach the B1116 again. Cross straight over passing a property called 'The Warrens' on the right and keep on over the next cross roads along a 'No Through Road'. You pass an extensive lake on your right and when the metalled lane turns off left you go with it passing the fine Georgian lines of Weybread House on the right.

Ignore a sandy track forking left up to a house and continue on the deteriorating metalled lane to a single property(SP, Bridleway)' Pass to the right of the red brick house and leave by a metal gate to continue along a grass track on the right side of a field with an area of woodland on your right. When the track ends continue along the right side of the field and at the end go over a metal gate on the right. Turn immediately left to carry on as before heading over a rough cart track and bridge towards farm buildings. Go over another metal gate and turn right to pass the almost windowless house on your left. Walk on, now along a firm track to meet the road at a footpath sign.

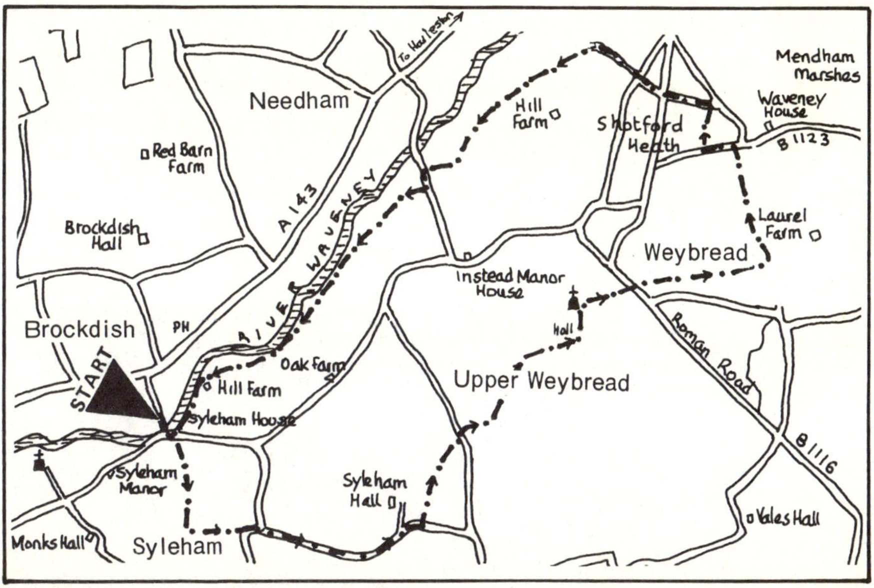

Turn left and carry on round the left hand bend and up the hill. Go over the metal farm gates on the right and head through a meadow. Carry on through the next along the bottom of the slope gradually bearing right. Half way across the next meadow where a hedge stops short coming down from your left, turn right and locate an open farm gate and rough cattle track heading into the trees. Take this track over an earthen bridge through a narrow section of meadow to a main bridge with metal handrails. Go onto the bridge which straddles the river Waveney and the counties of Norfolk and Suffolk.

Return back over the meadow, cross the earthen bridge and walk back up the cattle track out into the main meadow again. Turn immediately right and follow the cattle path. Bear right of a cross hedge and along a track used by cattle and often rather sticky - if it is wet, it is best to keep to the left. Go over a metal gate and keep on, bearing left of the trees ahead, to enter a wide grassy way between old hedges and trees. Go over another metal gate avoiding the wooden gate to the left. Soon an old grass path comes in from the left after you have passed through a wide opening in the hedge, here you bear slightly right to carry on beside the river.

After heavy rain, flooding of the river, or if cattle have been recently driven through, the next section can be very sticky. The river winds away and you emerge into open rough pasture. You see a bridge slightly to the right of straight ahead spanning the river, but you carry on to the end of the meadow and a metal farm gate. Go over the gate onto a track leading to the bridge. Turn left to walk a few yards to a small farm building.

Turn right here to enter another meadow over mobile metal fencing gates. Keep on ahead to the right of sections of old hedge and negotiate a wire fence ahead. When you come to the end of the meadow confronted by a hedge and ditch, go over the barbed wire fence on the left and immediately right through a single wooden swing gate and over a wooden footbridge. Carry on along a well-used path bordered by chainlink fencing on the left and trees on the right to reach the road. Turn right, and right again in Syleham to recross the bridge over the Waveney and return to your starting point.

Listen and long -
It hears the bells of many churches chime,
It has a pleasant time:
The trees that bow to it their branches strong,
Hide many birds that make its spring one song;
And orchard boughs let fall their flowery wealth,
To float away by stealth,
And land in tiny covers a mile below,
Or round and round the stems of rushes veer
Like snowy foam, but truly none is here,
So calmly gurgle on the waters clear
with endless flow.

RIVER LARK

And Suffolk! Thou has many a spot
Thus marked for immortality;
Which those who feel their worth, would not
Willingly, carelessly, let die;
Because the dead of days gone by
Have there done, suffer'd or enjoyed,
What lies in faithful memory
To snatch them from Oblivion's void.

NUMBER FOURTEEN - RIVER LARK

Places vistied:
Bury St Edmunds,
Fornham St Genevieve,
Culford, West Stow, Hengrave.
Distance: *8¼ miles (returning by road from West Stow is a similar distance)*
Starting Point: *Service Road opposite Gateway Supermarket and garage on the Mildenhall road out of Bury St Edmunds (the A1101).*
Refreshments: *Bury St Edmunds; shop at Culford.*
Map Ref: *1:25000 Pathfinder TL86/96, TL87/97*
1:50000 Landranger Sheet 155.

WEST STOW HALL GATEHOUSE

THE WALK: Cross the road and take the footpath beside the garage(SP) for about 200 yards to reach the banks of the river Lark where you turn left. The scruffy state of the path and surroundings one comes to expect this near town soon disperses, and the scenery becomes more enjoyable, though the golf course which straddles the river gives the landscape a rather artificial appearance. Watch out for flying golf balls where the tee is on one side of the path and the hole on the other!

At Sheepwash Bridge carrying the B1106 over the river, cross the road and continue on along the bank which is now very overgrown in places.

You are now passing through Fornham St Genevieve. The church was destroyed by fire in 1775 through the carelessness of a man shooting jackdaws on the thatched roof; the ruined tower still stands beyond the river. Along this stretch was the scene of the defeat of the Earl of Leicester's forces by Humphrey de Bohun in 1173. Supporting Henry II's sons in their rebellion against their father, Leicester had landed at Walton and after capturing the castle at Haughley, was on his way to the Midlands via Bury St Edmunds.

De Bohun, leading the King's forces, ambushed the rebels as they attempted to cross the river amidst much carnage; a ring found in the river was said to be that dropped by the fleeing Countess of Leicester.

Arriving at a footbridge with metal handrails, cross the river and continue on the right bank past Ducksluice Farm. Where the river takes a sweep to the left your route is straight on across rather marshy rough ground to pick up the wall again further on. Leave the river at the road bridge turning right along a narrow country lane.

After 500 yards turn left at a crossroads, and after another 400 yards, right along a track opposite Little Farm. When the track bears away you walk through the trees on the right, with the post and rail paddock fence on your right. Continue on until you pass the drive of a house on your left and enter the road through an opening in the garden boundary wall.

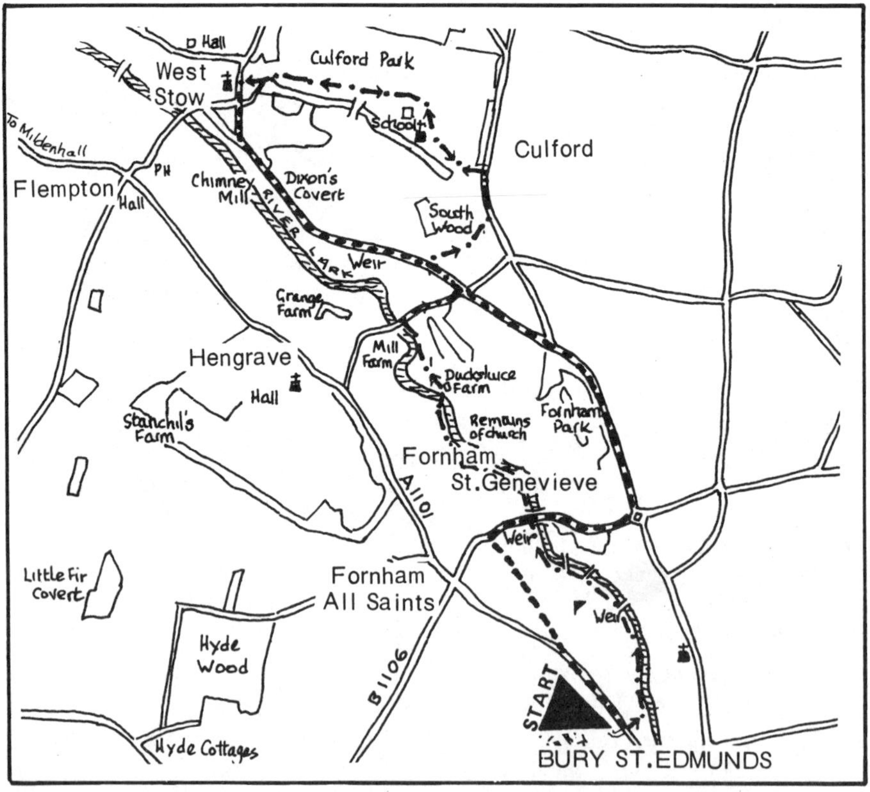

Turn left on the busy B1106; it is best to walk on the right side of the road where you will find a footpath. After about 300 yards, go through the side gate of the impressive entrance gates of Culford School on your left, and walk the metalled drive bearing right and left past the keeper's cottage on the right and the flint church of St Mary rebuilt in 1856 on the left set in pleasant parkland. At a 'roundabout' bear left to pass Culford Hall. The first hall was built by Nathaniel Bacon in 1591, while the present building of 1790 was the work of the first Marquess of Cornwallis. It is attributed to James Wyatt though it was enlarged out of all recognition around the turn of the century; the park was laid out by Repton. The Hall became a public school in 1935.

CULFORD HALL SCHOOL

You now have a pleasant walk of nearly ¾ mile through the park on the footpath. Just after reaching the lovely stretch of water on the left go through a gate in metal railings on the right and take the footpath through the trees to a quiet road opposite St Mary's church at West Stow.

It is not possible to link this walk by footpaths so to avoid a long journey by road I suggest retracing your steps back through Culford Park and back to the road bridge where you can rejoin the river wall and return to Bury St Edmunds and your starting point.

The alternative is to turn left at West Stow church and bear left at a fork after about 400 yards. Continue passing Dixon's Covert on your left for another 1½ miles to join the main B1106 road on a bend. After another ¾ miles turn right at a roundabout. Cross Sheepwash Bridge and after about 400 yards turn left.

You arrive at the A1101 Mildenhall road where you bear left and continue back to your starting point.

RIVER ALDE

With ceaseless motion comes and goes the tide
Flowing, it fills the channel vast and wide;
Then back to sea, with strong majestic sweep
It rolls, in ebb yet terrible and deep;
Here Samphire-banks and Salt-wort bound the flood
There stakes and sea-weeds withering on the mud;
And higher up, a ridge of all things base,
Which some strong tide has roll'd upon the place.

(George Crabbe)

NUMBER FIFTEEN - RIVER ALDE

Places visited: *Snape, Iken, Tunstall Forest.*
Distance: *7¼ miles*
Starting Point: *Car Park behind Snape Maltings.*
Refreshments: *Pub and Cafe at the Maltings.*
Map Ref: *1:25000 Pathfinder TM25/35, TM44/45 1:50000 Landranger Sheet 156.*

SNAPE MALTINGS CONCERT HALL

THE WALK: From the car park take the footpath by the river heading away from the Maltings. The bank becomes a causeway with water on either side. After about ¼ mile at a point where the bank is broken and you can go no further, turn back and retrace your steps.

Just before arriving back at the car park, take the well-worn path left, then bearing left and right before meeting a track at the hedge going left through a gateway. This is not an official path, but one regularly used by visitors to the Maltings. If you wish to keep to the official right of way, go past the car park and the Maltings buildings onto the B1069 and turn left. Just past the gate to Snape Bridge House, turn left along a track signposted to Iken Cliff. After passing the grounds of the house on your left meet the path coming in from the car park and continue on through the gateway.

Carry on for over ½ mile passing through several marshy sections with the Alde away over on your left. Walk along the top of a dyke with a deep ditch on your right and saltings on your left, to a point where the path turns sharp left with Iken Wood over on your right.

Follow the track left here along the bottom of the field then through into a meadow. Continue on to the end to reach an information board at Iken Cliff Picnic Site. Join a footpath signposted to the river and when a track comes in from the right, turn left to pass some cottages. Go down to the river and turn right to follow the bank. The picture here was not always so peaceful and serene. Once vessels engaged in the coal and corn trade used to berth at Iken Cliff where the firm Mingay & Rope had its coalyard, and voyage from the Alde to London and even Rotterdam.

Carry on by the 'beach' with the isolated Iken church in the distance ahead. Ignore the footpath sign right and carry on along the path until it finally turns away from the river by an inlet to lead you up wooden steps and between chain-link fencing out into a quiet country road to the right of a cottage.

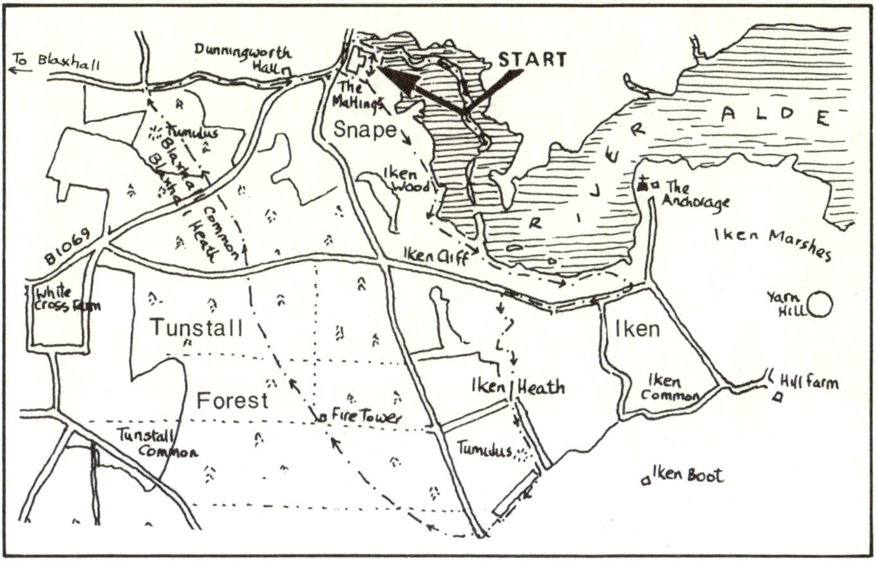

Turn right and continue for over ½ mile with lovely views over the river, passing the turning to Sandy Lane and later a track down to the farm on your left. Ignore the footpath sign right and eventually take one going left over a stile into a cultivated field. Walk down the right side of the field and at the bottom bear left for a few yards to leave through an opening in the fence and join a concrete drive to the left of farm buildings.

Go left for a few yards then right up a sandy track(SP) passing to the left of a pond. Walk up the right side of the field and at the top turn left(SP), then right (SP) to skirt the wood. The track swings right and left(SPs) to carry on now with the trees on your left. At the end of the field on your right, go just beyond the plantation of young fir trees and turn right(SP) to walk down the right side of the field with the plantation on the right. Just before the end of the field go right and left(SPs) to keep to the boundary and reach the road by a stile.

Cross the stile and turn right. Go a few yards round the bend and turn left over a wooden gate to take the woodland track into the mighty Tunstall Forest. Walk about 20 yards at right angles to the road and cross a track. After another 20 yards bear right at the fork and continue along a track for some ¾ mile ignoring all paths going off right and left, to reach a group of buildings. Head towards the Fire Tower and pass to the right to continue along Track 14 past an old Nissen hut.

Cross a road keeping to the track and after about 300 yards another track comes in from the left. At the three-way junction of paths take the left one into open heath. Keep on this sandy track to meet the B1069. Cross straight over and carry on for another 500 yards passing a tumulus on the left. A short distance after a track joins you from the left, you arrive at a country road.

Turn right and after a little over ½ mile meet the B1069 again near Dunningworth Hall. Carry on along this road back to the Maltings and your starting point.

There are refreshments here and plenty to see including an art gallery and craft shop. Boat trips are available along the Alde at certain times. The Maltings themselves form one of Europe's leading Concert Halls attracting leading artists from all over the world. It was destroyed by fire in 1969 but, due to its fame, rebuilt and open again a year later.

NUMBER SIXTEEN - RIVER ALDE/THE COAST

'HOUSE IN THE CLOUDS' & WINDMILL, THORPENESS

Places visited: *Aldeburgh, Thorpeness.*
Distance: *9½ miles*
Starting Point: *Car Park near the Coastguard Station beyond the High Street.*
Refreshments: *Ample in Aldeburgh; Dolphin Inn, Thorpeness.*
Map Ref: *1:25000 Pathfinder TM44/45 1:50000 Landranger Sheet 156.*

THE WALK: Climb the sea wall by the converted windmill, and head back towards Aldeburgh sea front; alternatively you can walk back along the road to the High

Street reaching the Moot Hall via a little back street beside the International Stores. Aldeburgh has been the home of the Internationally famed Aldeburgh Music Festival since 1948 along with its leading figures, Benjamin Britten and Peter Pears; another famous son was the poet George Crabbe whose writings immortalised much of the atmosphere of this coast.

The ancient Market Place has now been lost to the North Sea and you reach the beach via its only remaining building, the Moot Hall built around 1520. Turn north and head along the shore.

After 1½ miles houses on the outskirts of Thorpeness appear on the left beyond the beach and when, after another ¼ mile, you reach a point a little short of the end of the cliff line, turn left and head up the beach to leave by a track passing to the right of a pink coloured bungalow.

When you meet Beacon Hill Lane, turn left to head for the Dolphin Hotel in the distance. Bear left here onto the high road at a bend in front of the hotel. The brick gatehouse and timber-clad buildings on the right were the creation of Stuart Ogilvy in the early 1900's, as was the Mere you are now approaching.

After a few yards cross the road and take Stoney Lane by the footpath sign 'To the B1122' passing to the right of the Mere. When it approaches a T junction of tracks bear right along a well-worn path through the trees. You join the track again and bear right.

Eventually you arrive at the beautifully preserved post-windmill on the left and 'The House in The Clouds' on the right, two unique buildings standing side by side. The mill is of 1803 and brought here from Aldringham while the eccentric house is in fact an 85' high water tower on stilts, the tank disguised as a house; the role has been fully played out, the building now genuinely used as a private home.

At the Golf Course take the metalled drive, but as it bears left you carry on straight ahead along a footpath(SP). The Mere runs beyond the wooded areas on your left and in summer you may hear the holidaymakers paddling their little boats on the waters. You walk for a few yards along the edge of the golf course then continue on a well-used path.

You reach a set of delapidated level-crossing gates and turn left onto the disused railway track towards the wood. Carry on through the trees and when the track is blocked by a wire fence bear right along the main path into the North Warren Reserve which is under the RSPB. Continue on an attractive woodland walk, then along a grassy path through braken to reach the B1122.

Turn left onto this busy road and negotiate the next 700 yards or so with care. When you come to an unmade road on the left(SP) take it, passing several properties set in large grounds. You reach the old railway track again and cross a stile beside a metal farm gate to enter it. Turn right and walk for over ½ mile along this pleasant way, reclaimed from the railway by the Aldeburgh Society for public use.

At a point where you meet a modern bungalow on the right, leave the track by

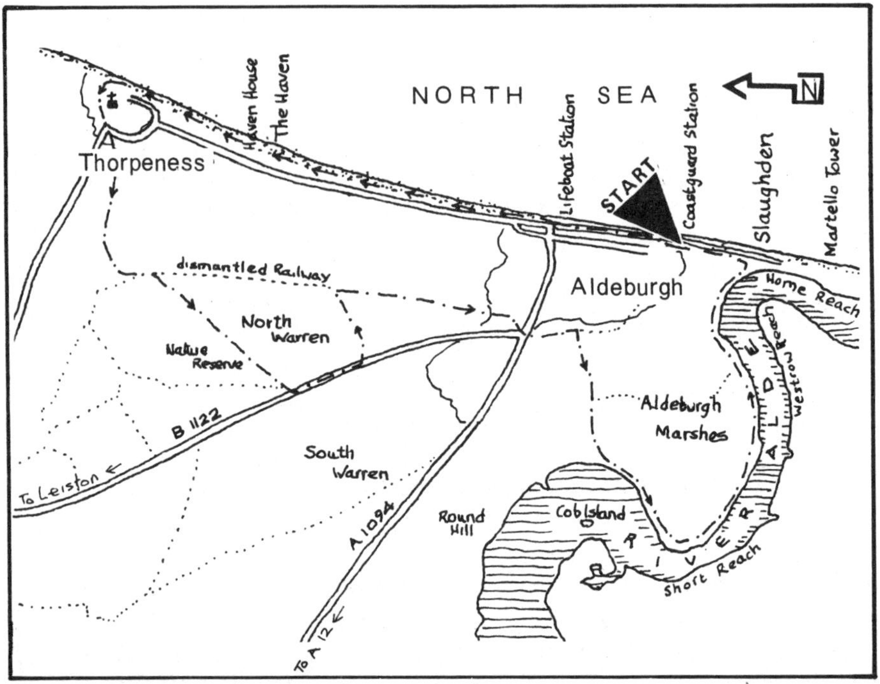

bearing left onto a path running parallel and taking you to a road junction on the outskirts of town. Fork right onto another well-trodden path for the last few yards to reach the junction opposite the unmade road leading to the fire station.

Cross the road and head towards the fire station. At the recreation ground continue straight ahead along a path beside a long brick wall. At the end take the path beside allotments and when you reach a gate on the right at a footpath sign, go through and head between the allotments towards the river wall ahead. Follow the directions, crossing several footbridges and stiles and eventually climb the grassy bank by the signpost.

Turn left and commence a 2 mile walk along the banks of the river Alde. The small island across the water at this point is Cob Island, while Aldeburgh Marshes on your left have now been drained and reclaimed for cultivation. You sweep left at Short Reach and further on pass the boats moored along Westrow Reach.

Ahead is Slaughdon, now only a thin penninsula of land between the Alde and the sea, but once a busy quay with houses and a pub; all have perished, the latter within this century. The Martello Tower, still with fine earthworks, was built between 1810-12 as a defence against a threatened invasion by Napoleon and is the northernmost Martello Tower in England.

When the river wall meets the sea wall go down and turn left to return to the car park and your starting point.

RIVER BLYTH

The bolder charms of savage scenery may,
Auspiciously beheld, demand delight;
Enforcing admiration, and delay,
Thy softer charms more willingly invite;
But though the former fill the roving sight
With mute astonishment; yet soon it grows
Sated with wonder, and, bewildered quite,
Longs for some scene on which it may repose,
Such scenes as thy sweet Banks so lavishly desclose.

(Bernard Barton)

NUMBER SEVENTEEN - RIVER BLYTH

Places visited: *Blythburgh, Wenhaston.*
Distance: *5½ miles*
Starting Point: *Car Park at Blythburgh Church.*
Refreshments: *White Hart and shop, Blythburgh; Pub and shop Wenhaston.*
Map Ref: *1:25000 Pathfinder TM47/57 1:50000 Landranger Sheet 156.*

BLYTHBURGH CHURCH

THE WALK: This comprises in the main, a walk along both banks of the river Blyth to Wenhaston and back. Though not long, the banks, especially in summer, are extremely overgrown, particularly the right bank on the outward journey, and as a result the walk can be very strenuous.

Come out of the car park into a narrow metalled lane and turn left. Bear right by a small green area and continue past two fine timber-framed houses, 'The Green' and, 'The Priory', in whose garden are the scanty remains of the Augustinian Priory founded in 1125. Arrive at the main A12 oppostie The White Hart public house an ancient building used as the Court House for the port of Blythburgh in medieval times.

Turn left and cross the Bridge, turning immediately left(SP) to go down to the river wall. You now face a 1½ mile walk along the right bank of the Blyth. As previously stated the going on this side of the river is very hard with long thick grass and, in summer, nettles and brambles covering a bank on which there are few signs of having been walked before.

At one point along the way you leave the wall by a stile and walk along the bottom of a sandy hill but when the wall reappears you must return to it.

Cross a track via two stiles and again negotiate two stiles at a bridge over the river. The large buildings away on your right at Bulcamp, comprise a hospital for the elderly. This was originally a workhouse, partly destroyed in a riot in 1766 and rebuilt. The church ahead is All Saints at Blyford.

At the next bridge cross the river and head along a pasture with a barbed wire fence on your right. Cross two streams dividing meadows by small bridges and at the end turn left and go through a gate. Take the next farm gate on your right into an earthen lane. At Holly Cottage bear left with the track and pass a farm on your right before bearing right on what becomes a firm stony track to a metalled road. Then right onto this and pass modern properties to arrive in Wenhaston near the church. You may need to turn right or left here in search of refreshments after your strenuous river walk, but the route goes straight over along a lane passing the entrance to St Peter's church.

Traces of a Saxon building were discovered at the restoration of the 13c. chancel of the church in 1892 but the main claim to fame here is the wonderfully preserved Last Judgement or 'Doom', painted on boards formerly sited above the chancel arch; it is 17' long by 8'6" high and was probably painted around 1500.

After visiting the church, continue along the lane which then becomes a well-worn path beside a cultivated field. When it branches at the end of the field at a triangle of grass, take the right fork and, within a few paces, leave the main track to branch right onto a narrow path heading towards a white cottage with a red tiled roof. Pass to the right of Grove View out onto the road.(SP).

Turn right and walk to the village centre where you bear left to join the road to Halesworth and Bungay passing Cobbles Cottage. Keep on the right side of the road past the track down to Vale Farm and head down the hill.

Immediately prior to the first property on the right, a modern bungalow, go over the stile on the right(SP) and walk along the edge of the field with the bungalow below the retaining wall on your left. Continue to the end of the field and go through the hedge. Turn right and at the end of the field on your left, just before entering the short length of overgrown farm track leading to Vale Farm, turn left and head up the field.

When you sight the tower of Blythburgh church on the horizon continue on in roughly this direction to locate a gap in the hedge on the far side of the field. Clamber through into the next field. Ahead beyond the end of the field is the lane you originally walked, with Holly Cottage on the left and the farm buildings on the right. Make for a point mid-way between the two where you should locate a gap in the hedge enabling you to reach the lane. Turn left and at Holly Cottage bear

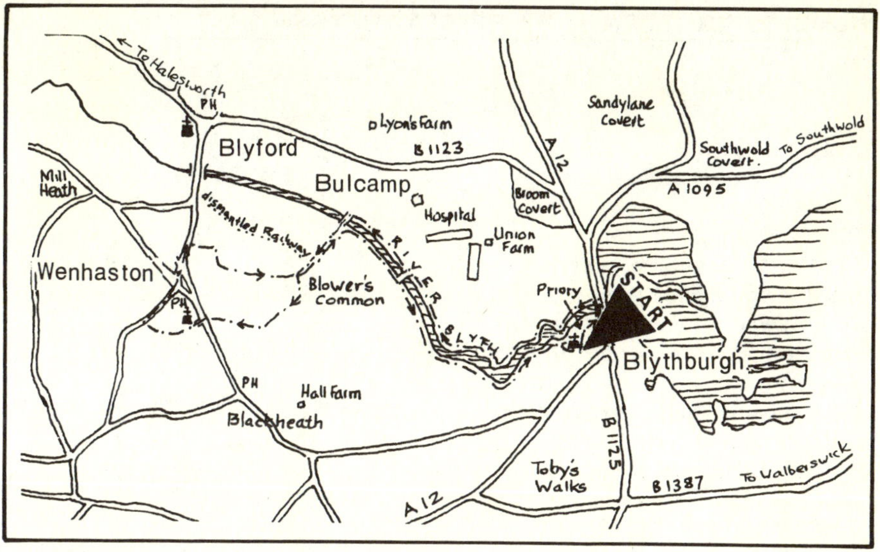

right. Go over the gate again, turning left to pass through the next and right to head back to the river bank via the two footbridges over the streams.

This time do not cross the bridge at the river, but turn right to pick up the near bank and head back towards Blythburgh. The going is slightly easier on this side where cattle have trodden a path and it will improve still further as you proceed. The stiles of the far bank have been replaced by barbed wire fencing, covered, to facilitate easy negotiation. When you round the hill on your left you will see the church ahead to give you encouragement. The river takes a wide sweep to the right and then finally arrives at Blythburgh where you leave the bank and walk across the grass. Turn right into a narrow grassy lane leading up to the small green and seat passed when you set out. Turn right into the churchyard for a visit to the church.

Holy Trinity is one of Suffolk's grandest churches. It is 128' long and has a tower 83' high. Until the year 1577 this was topped by a spire. Apart from the 13c. tower, most of the church is 15c., but the history of Blythburgh and its church go back much further than this. The Christian King Anna was buried here in a church of wood, thatch and mud following his defeat by the heathan Penda at nearby Bulcamp, while evidence of Ancient Britons and Imperial occupation have been unearthed in the vicinity. The interior of the church is high, light and spacious and the fine painted roof has carved wooden angels, some pitted with lead shot as a result of a visit from Dowsing's men during the Civil War.

Walk through the churchyard back to the car park and your starting point.

Places visited: *Walberswick, Southwold.*
Distance: *10½ miles (including 4 mile Southwold walk).*
Starting point: *Public car park in Walberswick Nature Reserve in the area of Tinker's Walks.*
Refreshments: *Bell Inn, Cafe and restaurant, Walberswick. Ample places in Southwold.*
Map Ref: *1:25000 Pathfinder TM47/57 1:50000 Landranger Sheet 156*

LIGHTHOUSE, SOUTHWOLD

THE WALK: From the car park walk along the right side of the trees of Sallow Walk Covert on your left to reach the B1387. Cross the road by Eastwoodlodge Farm and turn right. After a few yards take the footpath Left(SP) to walk diagonally over the heath. Cross over a track, and at cross paths turn left. After about 350 yards you meet the track again just before a house called Tinker's Barn. Cross it again and walk along a grass path heading through undergrowth to enter a cultivated field. Cross straight over the field and at the other side go through a gap in the hedge to join a farm track leading from the road and Eastwoodlodge Farm.

Turn right and when the track terminates at the derelict Tinker's House, turn left to walk along a green path. Go through the wire fence on the right into a meadow which you cross in the direction of the river wall. Meet a footpath sign here pointing your way along the bank.

Follow the winding course of the River Blyth for about 1¾ miles, the long grass and the lack of a clearly defined path making the going quite strenuous. Pass a delapidated windpump and, when the river divides, keep to the right to skirt a piece of isolated water.

You arrive at a stile by a bridge carrying a narrow metalled track over the river, where you have a choice; either cross the track by the stiles to continue on towards Walberswick or take the additional 4 mile walk round Southwold first.

For the full walk, turn left and cross the bridge to the Southwold side. Turn right and walk along the tow path on the left bank of the river past boats moored along the quay. Continue past the car park and the Harbour Inn, the Southwold Sailing Club Headquarters and the Lifeboat Station. Head along the harbour towards the beach and the point where the Blyth meets the sea - a spectacular sight in rough weather.

At the beach turn left passing the gleaming white tower of the lighthouse erected on North Green in 1886 away over on your left. Pick up the concrete promenade bordered by beach huts and later pass a number of wheeled bathing huts, such a feature of Victorian seaside photographs.

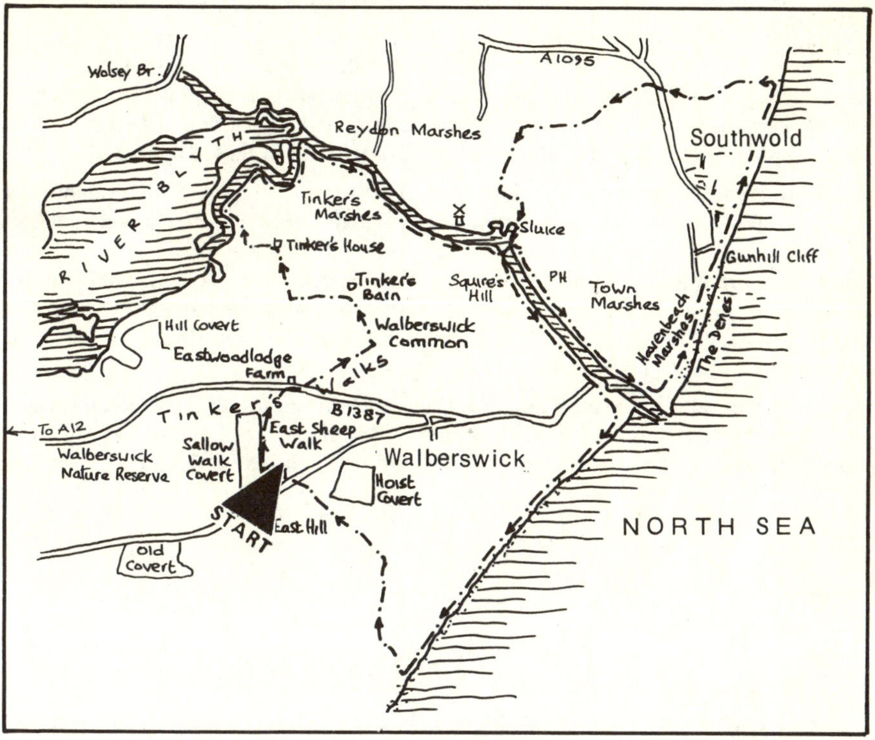

Arrive at the pier and walk out to the road. Carry on past the pier and car park, and a boating lake on the left. When confronted by fencing and a 'Private' notice board enclosing what remains of Easton Bravents, turn left and climb onto the river wall. This small parish of Easton Bravents situated on a high cliff is now almost totally beneath the waves of the North Sea; Easton Ness, now washed away, was England's most easterly point.

Carry on along the wall bordering Buss Creek with the boating lakes on your left. At a couple of places you may have to come down off the bank to skirt the concrete block defencive structures and, later, bushes. Go over a stile and eventually arrive at Mights Bridge carrying the only road into Southwold over the Creek. Cross stiles on either side of the road and carry on as before, now on the right bank.

You reach a stile and cross to a metalled path where you turn left over the water and immediately right again over another stile to continue on the left bank now short and mown. Over another fence carrying on in the same direction and ignoring paths going off left in the general direction of the water tower.

You finally arrive back at the bridge which you recross. Turn left over the stile to continue along the right bank of the Blyth towards Walberswick or, for an easier walk, along the tow path. At Walberswick, go between buildings and cross a wooden plank bridge to reach the beach. A short walk to the village from this point will enable you to visit The Bell for a well-earned drink and anything from a snack to a full meal.

Walberswick, now an attractive sea-coast village and a haunt for artists and fishermen, was once a place of much greater importance as its impressive but half-ruined church will testify. The encroachment of the sea and a decline in the fishing industry following the Reformation, brought about its sad demise.

Go down onto the beach and turn right. Leaving the little resort to its memories, continue along the beach for some 1½ miles in the direction of Dunwich. When you see a path coming in from the right beside a drainage channel leading to a derelict windpump, come down from the shingle bank and take this well-trodden route along a causeway through the Corporation Marshes; the large hill to your left is Dingle Great Hill surrounded by Dingle and Westwood Marshes, and the wood beyond, part of the great Dunwich Forest.

Pass the pump on your left and continue until the causeway ends. Keep straight on across the grass to join a track which will lead you to the road passing Hoist Covert on your right. Cross over the road and reach the car park and your starting point.

WALBERSWICK

RIVERS ORE & BUTLEY

A land that is lonelier than ruin;
A sea that is stranger than death:
Far fields that a rose never blew in,
Wan waste where the winds lack breath;
Waste endless and boundless and flowerless
But of marsh-blossoms fruitless as free:
Where earth lies exhausted, as powerless
To strive with the sea.

(Algernon Charles Swinburne)

NUMBER NINETEEN - RIVER ORE/BUTLEY RIVER

Places visited: *Boyton, Hollesley Bay.*
Distance: *8½ miles*
Starting Point: *Boyton Bell public house.*
Refreshments: *Boyton Bell.*
Map Ref: *1:25000 Pathfinder TM24/34 1:50000 Landranger Sheet 169.*

BUTLEY PRIORY

THE WALK: Leave the car park beside the Bell and turn left to walk back up the road to reach an S bend sign. Turn right here down a firm track and when it bears left, carry straight on left of a tree bearing a yellow footpath arrow. Go over a wooden gate following the arrow signs beside a paddock and stables, over a metal gate and across the meadow to a stile and footbridge. Carry on along a wide grass track going over a stile and passing to the right of a modern brick cowshed. Pass through a single wooden gate and head to the right of the post and rail fence to reach the road via the shingle drive of a farmhouse.

Turn right and walk to the crossroads where you take the road right signposted to Boyton passing red-brick farm buildings. The narrow country road bears left and right and when it turns sharp right, you bear left along a metalled lane.

The lane goes straight for some way then turns right between gates to cross an area known as Stonebridge Marshes. Pass in front of the sandy mound Burrow Hill, originally an island until the marshes were enclosed sometime in the 16c.; the hill must have been settled in Roman times as Latin scribes called it "Insula de Burg". The track bears right and left between a barn and Butley Ferry Farmhouse, where a ferry crossed to Orford. Climb over the farm gate and cross an area of meadowland by a grass path towards the river wall. Cross a culvert and stile to climb the bank and turn right.

The grass is short and the going easy as you set out along this 3¼ mile river walk beside first the Butley, and later the Ore. After ½ mile you pass the jetty at the end of a track leading from Dock Farm, and then Boyton Marshes on the right with two concrete structures standing unused and abandoned in the field, a remnant from World War II.

At a point where the wall turns right, stop and look ahead to Dove Point across the water. A little to the left is the lighthouse on Orford Ness and further left the church and castle at Orford itself. Continue on to Flybury Point where you bear right again to walk beside the river Ore.

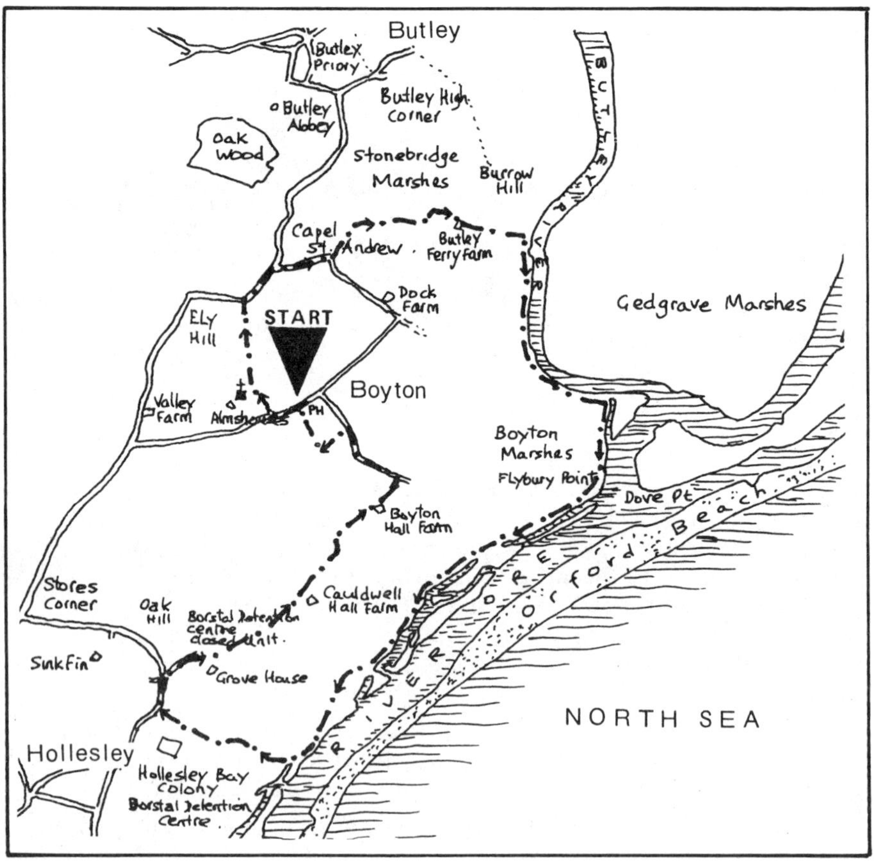

Beyond the river and running parallel is a shingle spit called Orford Beach which has built up and extended along the coast over the centuries to create the River Ore and completely cut off the important medieval port of Orford from the sea.

Further on you go over another stile and turn left with the wall, and then ignoring the path leading away from the river over the next stile, cross another ahead to skirt a pillbox sitting squarely on the wall. Cross two more stiles either side of a track and then go over a ramp leading to a small jetty; note the large modern block of buildings comprising the closed unit of Hollesley Bay Borstal Detention Centre away over to the right.

Reach another pillbox which you walk round to continue on a concrete wall. When it ends do not carry on over another stile, but come down off the bank and take the firm track through gates heading away from the river along the right side of a meadow. The farm track bears right and left and then right and left again. Now bordered by tall trees on the left, it turns right and leads past farm buildings out into the road by the entrance to Hollesley Bay Colony, the main buildings of the Borstal Detention Centre.

Turn right along the road and at a left hand bend, right again on a metalled drive leading to the Closed Unit noted earlier; there is also a 'Bridleway' sign here. When the drive, now concrete, turns into the unit, carry straight on along a firm dirt track with the high wire enclosure fencing on the left. The track develops a concrete surface as it passes the turning down to Cauldwell Hall Farm on the right, and later you pass the buildings and the farmhouse of Boyton Hall.

Turn left at the junction of tracks to walk a sunken way with high banks and hedges either side. When it turns right passing a delapidated barn on your left, it becomes a metalled lane. Take the green lane going off left(SP) on a left hand bend, and when it reaches a cottage, turn right to follow a dirt track between open fields. Pick up a hedge on your right and continue to the end where you find two caravans. Pass to the right of the small scruffy one standing end on, to pass along a narrow path bordered by high hedging on the right and low iron railings on the left. You come out into the road by a footpath sign, turn right and walk the few yards back to the pub and your starting point.

THE COAST

. . . . Who still remains to hear the ocean roar,
Whose greedy waves devour the lessening shore;
Till some fierce tide, with more imperious sway,
Sweeps the low hut and all it holds away;
When the sad tenant weeps from door to door,
And begs a poor protection from the poor.

(George Crabbe)

NUMBER TWENTY – THE COAST AT MINSMERE

Places visited: *Eastbridge, Dunwich, Minsmere.*
Distance: *8 miles*
Starting Point: *Layby near the Minsmere River bridge just north of Eastbridge.*
Refreshments: *Ship Inn and snack bar, Dunwich; Eels Foot public house, Eastbridge.*
Map Ref: *1:25000 Pathfinder TM44/45, TM46 1:50000 Landranger Sheet 156.*

WESTLETON

THE WALK: From the layby walk over the bridge and after ¼ mile turn right along a track through the trees. Continue on through the Minsmere Nature Reserve and Westleton Walks. After ¾ mile you arrive at an unmade road with a 'Private Road' sign on the right, cross straight over signposted 'Bridlepath' and take a narrow but well-used path into Scottshall Coverts.

After about 400 yards the main path bears right signposted to Minsmere, but you carry straight on along a wide grassy lane bordered by heather. It reverts to a narrow path through overgrown bushes but is still well-trodden and clearly defined. Meet a track coming in from the left and join it to continue on ahead. The track soon turns off right but you carry on along a narrow path to eventually reach the road.

Cross over and continue on the path through the woods(SP), passing to the left of an old bungalow and caravan. Cross a track and when the path forks bear right. Come out across a lawn to join an unmade road. Turn left and pass several properties before reaching a road.

Turn right and when the road bends left after a short distance you carry on(SP) along another unmade road bordered by houses. The road becomes a track as you pass the last cottage on the left, and when it divides at a signpost of footpaths, turn left - the sunken way ahead towards the low bridge is the remains of one of Dunwich's old medieval streets.

As your own track approaches the road it is bordered on the right by the old flint wall surrounding Greyfriars Priory and, when you turn right and walk along the road towards the village itself, you pass the impressive 13c Gateway and are able to peep through at the sparce remains within, standing forlorn amid grazing sheep.

When the road bends left at the Ship Inn you have a choice of refreshments. If the pub is open they will provide you with a drink, snack or meal, while your route takes you right at the bend to a car park and snack bar by the beach.

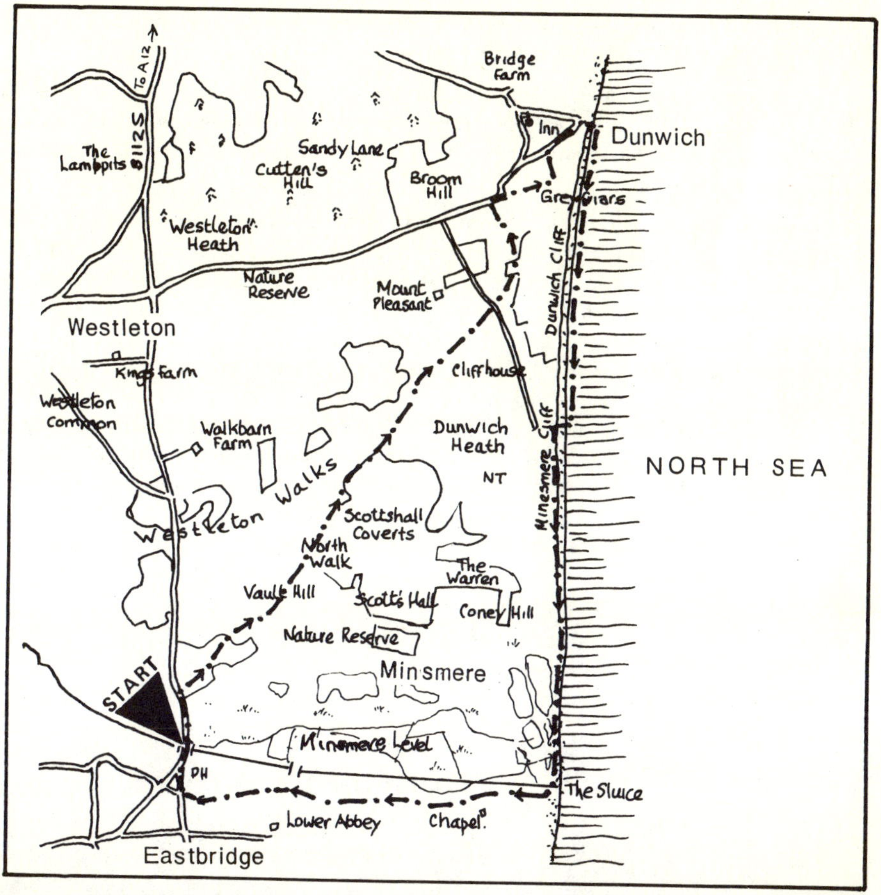

The car park occupies the site of Maison Dieu one of Dunwich's hospitals which like the rest of this medieval city has disappeared, most of it beneath the waves. Turn right and head along the beach keeping clear of the crumbling cliffs which are unstable and always liable to collapse. The last structure to go over the cliff was All Saints Church which fell to the beach in 1904, its tower following in 1921; during my last walk here some small sections of flint walls were exposed at low tide.

After nearly 1½ miles and after passing two sets of steps climbing the cliff (the first providing access to a caravan site and the other to a house and sporting a 'Private, No Entry' sign), take the next wooden steps to reach the top of the cliff. Carry on along the cliff path to the car park.

Continue on past the car park where there is a choice of two wide green paths to follow, one a sunken way which looks more like a disused railway track. The large white building ahead to the right is the coastguard station. When you reach the start of a line of Second World War concrete tank defences, pass them on your left and carry on with wooden Bird Reserve hides interspersed on the right - the Reserve itself is only accessable to permit holders.

When you arrive at a large concrete sluice gate, turn right over a wooden gate, to head away from the sea following the course of the drainage channel. Over the next gate and stile you come down the bank and bear left as directed by the footpath sign on the gate.

Look across the cultivated field on your left to the remains of an ancient chapel, sole surviving remnant from the original premonstratensian Abbey built too near the sea and moved to its present site at Leiston in 1363.. Carry on over further gates, and when confronted by two side by side, go over the one to the right. Further along bear left and right over another gate. The wide dirt track is used by cattle and during wet weather can be very sticky. Finally when the track turns left and you meet several gates, go left then right over a stile into a cultivated field. Head straight up the middle of the field along a usually well-defined path and at the end carry on through a short section of rough ground. Continue along the right side of two more fields, then the path turns right at the garden gate of Boundary Cottage and left onto a track leading to the road. Pass the gates to Holly and Mere Cottages and reach the road opposite the telephone kiosk. Turn right and pass the houses in the hamlet of Eastbridge and the Eels Foot pub to reach the layby near the bridge and your starting point.

Places visited: *Alderton, Shingle Street.*
Distance: *5½ miles*
Starting Point: *Turn left at the right hand bend in the centre of Alderton and park in the area of Watsons Way just out of the main village.*
Refreshments: *Alderton Swan*
Map Ref: *1:25000 Pathfinder TM24/34 1:50000 Landranger Sheet 169.*

ALDERTON

THE WALK: Walk back towards Alderton village and take the cinder track left to 'Shingle Street 2 miles'. The track passes between properties and a playing field on the left to become a well-worn path beside the hedge with a field on the right. Do not take the concrete track going off right but continue straight ahead between fields and then with a field on the left and a stream on the right. Go over a wooden footbridge and turn right with the stream. Carry on along the left bank and bear left avoiding the concrete bridge. Keep on to pick up the sea wall which you climb and turn left.

Pass by the Martello Tower on your left and just past a footpath sign directing walkers both ways along the wall, go down the right side of the bank. Walk over and cross the stile leading into a meadow keeping roughly parallel with the wall, then head diagonally across to the far right hand corner to leave by a wooden swing gate passing between a bungalow on your right and another Martello Tower on your left.

You have arrived at Shingle Street, a desolate expanse of coastline with a scattering of weather-beaten buildings huddled together in defiance of the elements.

The Martello Towers took their name from Sir David Dundas following his experience in Corsica where a round tower on Point Mortella with walls 18' thick had succeeded in driving off several men-of-war. The towers along the English coast were not as substantial having been built in rather a panic when an invasion by Napoleon seemed imminent; the South Coast was given priority, those on what was considered the less vulnerable East Coast not being completed until about 1812. Each tower required some 700,000 bricks, some of which were made locally, had an average diameter of 26', walls 9' thick at the front and 5' at the rear and a height of about 34'. Like the pillboxes and tank defences of the two World Wars, they were never needed but stand as a reminder to those of us today experiencing the threat of Nuclear war, that fear of war and invasion has been a cross our forefathers also had to bear.

Look out to sea and the end of the shingle spit - this was created when nature and gales wiped out two-thirds of Aldeburgh and spread a ridge of shingle down the coast cutting off the medieval port of Orford.

Continue along the beach and leave just past the old Coastguard Station to pick up a firm drive heading towards an isolated property ahead. When you come level with this single storey building, turn left and walk across the grass along a faint path to the river wall(SP). Climb the bank and turn right to carry on in the same direction as before; if the bank becomes too overgrown to walk, a short grass path develops down on the right side of the bank.

When the wall turns away from the sea follow it and cross a stile. Carry on, the going much easier with water on either side to another stile by the road.

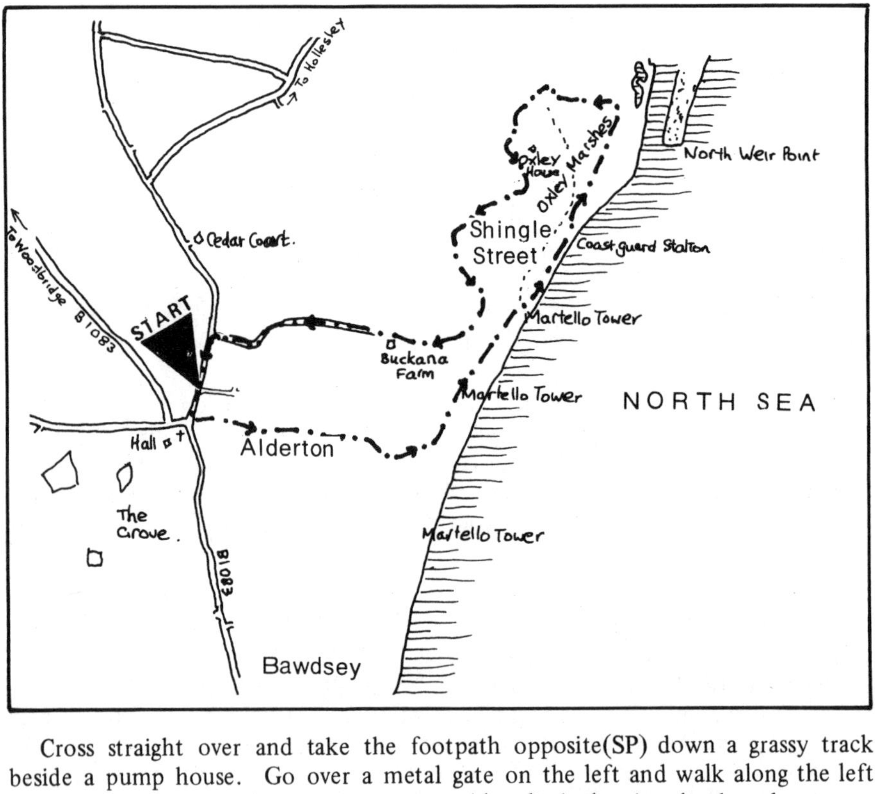

Cross straight over and take the footpath opposite(SP) down a grassy track beside a pump house. Go over a metal gate on the left and walk along the left bank of the stream. As soon as you are able, climb the river bank and carry on along the top - the grass is short and the way well-trodden by cattle; where confronted by bushes you will have to drop down the bank on the left to skirt them. Climb a set of wooden steps to negotiate a wire cattle fence. The grass becomes longer and tougher but progress should be steady. Take a wide sweep to the right and then head for the Martello Tower you skirted on your outward trip. When a length of bank bears away left over a stile towards the tower, you carry straight on. You reach the point where you left the wall earlier and this time come down the bank on the right by a telegraph pole.

Cross the culvert over the stream and head away from the wall and the sea across the field following the line of the telegraph poles until you meet a firm farm track. Bear right onto this and head for the farm buildings. Pass a pillbox and bear right and left to reach the farmyard. Continue on the track past grain silos and leave the farm buildings of Buckanan Farm on the left as you head away on what becomes a metalled lane.

After about ¾ mile follow the S bend past a modern bungalow on your left to arrive at the road on a T junction. Opposite is a small pillbox hidden in the hedge, nicely positioned, it was hoped, to give a rude awakening to those Nazi 'storm troopers' jauntily making their way up from a beach landing at Shingle Street; Which side would have had the greater shock is pure conjecture! The structure still has its original metal doors and its round design is unusual in this part of the country.

Turn left and walk back to Alderton and Watsons Way, your starting point.

SHINGLE STREET

SELECTED BIBLIOGRAPHY

The Suffolk Garland
Orwell Estuary, the story of Ipswich River - W. G. Arnott
Suffolk Villages - Allan Jobson
Rivers of East Anglia - James Turner
Selections from the Poems of Bernard Barton
Alde Estuary - W. G. Arnott
Suffolk Estuary - W. G. Arnott
The Suffolk Stour - Ambrose J. R. Waller
East Anglia from the Sea - David & Joan Hay
The Buildings of England (Suffolk) - Nikolaus Pevsner
Suffolk - P. G. M. Dickinson
Ipswich Through the Ages - Lillian Redstone
Suffolk - Norman Scarfe